Introduction

The Armistice of November 1918 that brought the First World War to a close was followed by the swift and dramatic collapse of the industries that had sustained Germany's war machine through four and a half years of conflict.

Of the aircraft constructors whose fighter designs had come close to sweeping the skies over Western Europe, the hardest hit was the Pfalz Flugzeugwerke, which had the misfortune to be located at Speyer airfield in southwest Germany and consequently came within the French zone of occupation. Stripped of all its assets, it managed to survive for some years by turning to other commercial activities, but eventually went bankrupt during the Great Depression of 1932.

The Albatros Flugzeugwerke, based at Johannisthal near Berlin, survived in the post-war world as an aircraft manufacturer by producing trainers and light aircraft until 1931, when it merged with the Focke-Wulf company and inherited Albatros's talented chief engineer and test pilot Kurt Tank, who embarked on a design path that would lead to the excellent Focke-Wulf Fw 190 fighter.

Dutchman Anthony Fokker, whose fighter designs had been the scourge of the air war since 1915, following the appearance of his Fokker monoplane with its synchronized forward-firing gun, escaped from a defeated Germany and re-established his company in his native Netherlands. After his company's relocation, Fokker continued to supply military aircraft to the Royal Netherlands Air Arm and various foreign air forces. He also turned to the design of commercial aircraft, and by the end of the 1920s he had become the world's largest aircraft manufacturer.

In June 1919 the Treaty of Versailles had imposed draconian restrictions on Germany, which was forbidden to manufacture or import aircraft of any kind for six months following the signing of the Treaty, or to have an air force. In 1922, after these restrictions were relaxed somewhat, gliding clubs and sports aviation clubs sprang up all over Germany with the support of the government; a secret military flying school was established at Lipetsk in the Soviet Union, its object to train a cadre of aircrew and technicians who would form the nucleus of a future Luftwaffe.

Within this more relaxed environment several new aviation manufacturing companies were founded. They included the Heinkel company, set up at Warnemünde

Willy Messerschmitt, pictured in later years, learned his trade by designing gliders, as did many other aircraft manufacturers.

in 1922 by Ernst Heinkel, who had been chief designer for the Hansa-Brandenburg aviation firm during the war, the Dornier Flugzeugwerke, founded by Claude Dornier and specializing in the production of large flying boats from 1923, and Junkers of Dessau, a long-established firm which now built all-metal commercial monoplanes.

And there was a young man called Wilhelm Emil 'Willy' Messerschmitt, who before the war had spent his spare time assisting a pioneer glider designer, Friedrich Harth. Both men resumed their gliding activities on completion of their military service, entering their designs in the competitions that were being held all over the country. In 1921 Messerschmitt designed the first of his own gliders, the tailless S9. The prize money won in the competitions enabled Harth and Messerschmitt to set up their own flight training school in 1922 but the venture was short-lived. Harth began to criticize Messerschmitt's design work, claiming that the junior partner's design input resulted in the gliders being unstable in flight. In the end the partnership was dissolved in 1923.

Messerschmitt founded his own aircraft company, the Flugzeugbau Messerschmitt, and set about designing powered aircraft. The first was the M-17, a lightweight all-wood sports aircraft powered by a British Bristol Cherub 29hp air-cooled engine. In September 1926, pilot Eberhard von Conta

Messerschmitt's M-17, seen here in replica form, was his first venture into powered aircraft.

The Messerschmitt M-18 was a popular aircraft. This example was operated by the Swiss Land Registry.

and a passenger, the writer Werner von Langsdorff, flew the little aircraft from Bamberg to Rome, marking the first time the central Alps were crossed by a light aircraft. The flight lasted fourteen hours, with three refuelling stops en route, and the M-17 reached an altitude of 4,500m (14,760ft). Messerschmitt, who had learned to fly in 1925, nearly lost his life while piloting an M-17, suffering a crash that hospitalized him for some time. Despite this setback, both the M-17 and its successor, the M-18, boosted the reputation of Messerschmitt's fledgling company immensely, and he went into business together with Theodor Croneiss, an ace who had gained five victories on the Ottoman Front. They saw an immediate opportunity for expansion when the state-owned airline Deutsche Luft Hansa was formed in 1926, setting up a 'feeder' service, the Nordbayerische Verkehrsflug, to fly to the airports that Luft Hansa served, using four-seater Messerschmitt M-18s.

Messerschmitt was now faced with a dilemma. He had orders for both the M-17 and M-18, but no money with which to buy the necessary construction materials. As a means of solving the problem, He approached the Bavarian government, which set up a deal involving the merger of his company with the Bayerische Flugzeugwerke (Bavarian Aircraft Works, or BFW) of Augsburg, which was in financial trouble. The arrangement was that BFW would limit

Messerschmitt was hard hit by the cancellation of orders for his M-20 airliner following a succession of accidents.

itself to the production of Messerschmitt's designs, relinquishing independent design work, while Messerschmitt agreed to give BFW first priority in the development of his new types. The two companies were consequently to retain their individuality, while pooling their economic resources. In practice, the deal gave Messerschmitt access to a large manufacturing facility and added a number of highly skilled workers to his workforce. A formal agreement was reached on 8 September 1927, and Messerschmitt moved his operations from Bamberg to Augsburg.

Messerschmitt's commercial future now seemed assured and he proceeded with another design, the ten-seat M-20. It was to prove his undoing. The prototype crashed on its first flight on 26 February 1928, killing its pilot, Hans Hackman. Despite this accident, which was found to have been caused by the fabric covering the wing trailing edges becoming detached, construction of more M-20s went ahead and deliveries to Luft Hansa began, but further orders were cancelled after the M-20 was involved in two more serious crashes, one of which killed eight senior officers of the Reichswehr, the German Army. Although this resulted in the cancellation of further M-20 orders by Luft Hansa, Messerschmitt persevered with his civil designs, which included the M-21 two-seat trainer, the M-22 twin-engine mailplane, the M-23 two-seat touring monoplane, and the M-24 eight-passenger transport. However, these did not attract enough interest to warrant quantity production, and by the end of 1929 BFW found itself in financial difficulty, despite receiving development subsidies. In June 1931 it went into receivership.

This did not affect Messerschmitt, which had retained its status as an independent company. In 1932, with the co-operation of the administrator, Messerschmitt attempted to reinstate BFW, and accommodations were reached with most of the creditors, and in May 1933 BFW began trading again under Messerschmitt's direction. It was at this juncture that Erhard Milch, who had been appointed Secretary of State for Air in the new Nazi government, made his dislike of Willy Messerschmitt clear by stating that he would not support the rejuvenated BFW company, insisting that it should concern itself solely with the licence manufacture of aircraft developed by other firms.

For Messerschmitt, who needed to produce his own designs to meet German contracts, it was a highly unsatisfactory state of affairs, but in the summer of 1933 a light appeared on the horizon when the Air Ministry decided to participate in the Challenge de Tourisme Internationale, a contest for sports aircraft. In view of Messerschmitt's experience in designing such types he was instructed to design and build an aircraft to compete in the event. The aircraft, a four-seat-cabin, low-wing monoplane, was the first of its size to feature all-metal, stressed-skin construction. It also had a retractable undercarriage.

The aircraft carried the company designation M-37. It would become better known to the world as the Messerschmitt Bf 108.

The Bf 108 successfully bridged the gap between the F4 44 biplane trainer, seen here at a parade of Luftwaffe recruits, and the Bf 109.

Origins of the Bf 109

Bf 108

The Bf 108 was a radical departure from anything previously attempted by the Messerschmitt design team. A low-wing, cantilever monoplane, it featured a trapezoidal wing, a short, low-aspect ratio configuration resulting in a thin wing with low drag at high speed while maintaining high strength and stiffness. It featured both leading and trailing edge spars, the whole covered with smooth metal sheet. The wing was fitted with leading edge slats, designed to maintain aerofoil efficiency at high angles of attack. The all-metal fuselage was of monocoque stressed-skin construction. First flown in the spring of 1934, the prototype Bf 108 was a two-seat aircraft. A small production batch was produced, these aircraft being designated Bf 108A. They were followed by the definitive production version, the Bf 108B, which was a four-seater.

The Bf 108B went on to be built in large numbers, both in Germany and later in Occupied France. It shared so many characteristics with the Bf 109 that it came to be widely used as an advanced and conversion trainer, bridging the gap between primary trainers like the Fw 44 and the fighter. The use of the Bf 108 also got pilots used to operating a retractable undercarriage, thereby reduced the number of landing errors made by pilots who, progressing to the Bf 109 from fixed-undercarriage fighters, forgot to lower their landing gear.

Bf 109: Design and Development

Although Messerschmitt still had his detractors, he had also acquired new supporters, the most influential of whom was Hermann Göring, who had replaced Milch as Secretary of State for Air and given the task of establishing the new Luftwaffe. Together with three other companies, the Ernst Heinkel AG, the Focke-Wulf Flugzeugbau and the Arado Flugzeugwerke, BFW was invited to enter a design competition to develop a new monoplane fighter. To meet the challenge, Messerschmitt assembled a talented design team. As his right-hand man and head of the design office he picked Walter Rethal, who had previously worked for Arado and who had experience in fighter design going back to the First World War. Then there was Robert Lusser, who had played a key part in the design of the Bf 108 and who would later be put in charge of

A beautifully restored Bf 108B pictured in flight over the Alps.

designing a new twin-engine heavy fighter, the Bf 110.

Design work on the monoplane fighter began in March 1934, just three weeks after a development contract was issued. In order to obtain the best possible performance, the design team elected to build the lightest and smallest possible airframe around the most powerful aero engine under development in Germany at the time, the 610hp Junkers Jumo 210A. The design incorporated many features of the proven Bf 108, including the leading edge slats to provide effective aileron control near the stall, and slotted flaps to reduce landing speed.

Initially designated Bf 109A, the aircraft that emerged was a cantilever low-wing monoplane built of metal with a flush-riveted duralumin skin. The fuselage was an elegant oval-section monocoque structure with an enclosed cockpit, the canopy opening sideways on hinges. The narrow-track undercarriage, designed so that the weight of the aircraft would be borne by the fuselage, retracted outward into the wing. The first prototype, bearing the civil registration D-IABI, was completed at the end of May 1935 but did not fly until mid-September and was fitted with an imported 695hp Rolls-Royce Kestrel engine, as the Jumo 210A twelve-cylinder inverted-V liquid-cooled engine was not yet available. It was now officially known as the Bf 109 V1, the letter V denoting Versuchs (Experimental). A second aircraft, the Bf 109 V2 (D-IUDE), was completed in October 1935 and was powered by the long-awaited Jumo 210A.

In February 1936 the Bf 109 V2 was sent to the military aviation test and development facility at Travemünde, on the Baltic coast, for comparative trials with the other contenders for the Luftwaffe contract: the Arado Ar 80 V3, the Focke-Wulf Fw 159 V3, and the Heinkel He 112 V4. The trials showed that the Bf 109 and He 112 were superior to the others, and the RLM placed an order for ten further examples of each aircraft for testing and evaluation.

The Bf 109 V2, which had provision for two 7.9mm Rheinmetall-Borsig MG 17 machine guns mounted in the forward upper fuselage ahead of the cockpit and synchronized to fire through the propeller disc was intended to form the basis of the planned first production model, the Bf 109A, but a change in the RLM requirement resulted in the Bf 109B, which was essentially the Bf 109 V4 fourth prototype (D-IOQY) fitted with a three-gun armament, a third MG 17 being mounted centrally in the engine compartment and firing through the propeller boss. Each MG 17 had 500 rounds of ammunition, but this was later increased to 1,000 rounds.

Meanwhile, examples of a 20mm drum-fed cannon, the MG FF, developed by the Swiss firm Oerlikon, had become available and one was tested in the Bf 109 V4,

Hermann Göring, seen during his early membership of the Nazi Party in 1925, gave Messerschmitt his full support.

The Bf 109 was intended to replace the Luftwaffe's biplane fighters such as the Arado Ar 68, seen here, and the Heinkel He 51.

A formation of Heinkel He 51 fighters.

The Arado Ar 80, despite its fixed undercarriage, was a contender in the contest for a new monoplane fighter.

The Messerschmitt Bf 109 V4 fourth prototype, D-IOQY, in flight.

A lineup of factory-fresh Bf 109B-1 fighters.

replacing the centrally mounted MG 17. However, it was found to have an unacceptably slow rate of fire and limited ammunition storage in its drums. It also produced a high level of vibration, so the armament configuration was modified and tested in the Bf 109 V8. The engine-mounted cannon was deleted and an additional MG 17 was mounted in each wing, outboard of the propeller disc, so that they did not need to be synchronized.

Two wing-mounted MG FF cannon were experimentally fitted in the Bf 109 V9, but the vibration problem occurred again, and the armament of four MG 17s was selected as standard for the Bf 109C production aircraft.

The main attraction of the MG FF, apart from its hitting power, was that it was compact and light, so the Ikaria Werke of Berlin, which was about to undertake licence production of the weapon, adapted it to fire a new type of high-capacity, high-explosive shell called Minengeschoss (Mine Shell). This had thinner walls than previous shells, permitting an increased explosive charge. It was also lighter and produced less recoil than earlier projectiles, which went a long way toward eliminating the vibration problem. In its new guise it was called the MG FF/M. The Bf 109 V14, D-IRTT, which flew in the summer of 1938, had two MG FF cannon in the wings and two nose-mounted MG 17 machine guns. The Bf 109 V15 also had two MG 17s, but only one 20mm FF cannon.

It was the Bf 109V-7, armed with two machine guns and a single MG FF cannon that became the pattern aircraft for the pre-production model, the Bf 109B-0, powered by a 610hp Jumo 210B engine. Willy Messerschmitt had originally intended the 109's thin wing to be left free of guns, but when the Luftwaffe High Command learned that the British Spitfire and Hurricane were to be fitted with eight machine guns they insisted that the Bf 109 was to carry wing-mounted guns too. Messerschmitt's reluctant response was to design a new wing, with bulges for the ammunition boxes of the 20mm cannon mounted on each side.

To cope with the expected Bf 109 production demands construction of a new factory was begun at Regensburg, the Augsburg facility being fully occupied with production of the Bf 108 and the completion of orders on behalf of other companies, a task dictated by the RLM. The new factory at Regensburg, completed in 1937, meant that BFW could concentrate solely on the Bf 109. The first production model, the Bf 109B-1, was fitted with the 635hp Junkers Jumo 210D engine, driving a fixed-pitch, two-blade wooden propeller. This was replaced at an early stage by the Hamilton two-blade variable-pitch metal propeller, which was fitted to the Jumo 210E engine installed in the Bf 109B-2. This engine, in turn, was quickly supplanted by the 670hp Jumo 210G.

In July 1937 five Bf 109s – two Bf 109B-1s, a Bf 109B-2, the Bf 109 V10 (D-ISLU) and the Bf 109 V13 (D-IPKY), the latter pair fitted with the new 960hp DB 600 engine – formed the German team that took part in an international flying meeting held at Dübendorf, Switzerland. Although there was an early setback when the Bf 109 V10 crashed after an engine failure (its pilot Ernst Udet walking away from the wreck), the international circuit of the Alps race was won by team leader Major Hans Seidemann in the Bf 109B-2, which also captured the speed event with Dipl Ing Carl

A lineup of factory-fresh Bf 109B-1 fighters.

A Messerschmitt Bf 109C-1.

Francke at the controls; the climb and dive contest was won by Dipl Ing Francke in the Bf 109 V13, and the team race was won by the Bf 109B-1s and the B-2, the aircraft being flown by Hauptmann Werner Restemeier, Oberleutnant Hannes Trautloft and Oberleutnant Fritz Schleif.

On 11 July, 1938, BFW was renamed Messerschmitt AG. Despite the name change, the prefix 'Me' only being applied to aircraft designed subsequent to the change in the company's name (e.g. Me 208, Me 209, Me 210.) The official RLM aircraft type specifications retained the Bf prefix for all production versions of the 109 throughout the war, as did all other official publications. The Me prefix was used by the Luftwaffe, but only unofficially.

The next Bf 109 production model was the Bf 109C-0, which was based on the V9 and had four MG 17 machine guns, two in the forward fuselage and two in the wing roots. The Bf 109C-1 was similar, but the C-2 mounted five MG 17s. The Bf 109 V11 and V12 prototypes were both fitted with production 960hp DB 600A engines, boosting their maximum speed to 520kph (323mph). These prototypes were the precursors of the Bf 109D production model, which had a 960hp DB 600Aa engine, two MG 17 machine guns and an engine-mounted FF cannon. The first production BF-109Ds were converted from Bf 109B airframes.

By the end of 1939, Bf 109 production had switched to the variant that was to remain the Luftwaffe's principal single-engine fighter for the next two years: the Bf 109E. A batch of ten pre-production Bf 109E-0 aircraft was followed by the initial production version, the Bf 109E-1; both were armed with four 7.92mm machine

A Heinkel He 70, showing its distinctive elliptical wing, flanked by Heinkel He 51s. Bf 109s can be seen at the far side of the snow-covered parade square. The aircraft in the background are Siebel Fh 104 Hallore light transports. The photograph was probably taken in 1938, the occasion being a passing-out parade of aircrew trainees.

One criticism of the Bf 109 was its cramped cockpit, which could make life difficult for bigger pilots.

A Bf 109E-1 pictured during a test flight.

guns. The fighter differed from earlier models in that it was powered by an 1,100hp Daimler-Benz DB 601A engine featuring direct fuel injection instead of a carburettor, ensuring that the motor did not cut out under negative 'g' conditions, a problem that plagued the early versions of the Rolls-Royce Merlin engine that powered the RAF's Spitfires and Hurricanes.

The Bf 109E-1 was fitted with the Funkgerät 7 (FuG 7) VHF radio equipment, effective over a range of 48–56km (30–35 miles). The Bf 109E-1/B was a fighter-bomber variant, fitted with racks for 50kg (110lb) SC 50 bombs under the wings or a single 250kg (550lb) SC 250 bomb under the fuselage. This variant used the Bf 109's Revi (Reflexvisier) reflector gunsight as a bomb sight, and the angle of dive was indicated by a red line painted on either side of the cockpit at 45° to the horizon. For bombing from low and medium altitudes the recommended diving speed was 600kph (373mph), while for high-altitude bombing the recommended diving speed was 648kph (403mph). The maximum permissible diving speed was 718kph (446mph). Of the 1,183 Bf 109E-1s built in total, 110 were E-1Bs.

The next sub-variant, the Bf 109E-2, was developed from the V20 prototype and armed with two MG FF cannon mounted in the wings and one in the engine, as well as two MG 17 machine guns mounted in the nose. After a short production run the emphasis switched to the Bf 109E-3, developed from the V16 and V17 prototypes. It was armed with two nose-mounted MG17 machine guns and an MG FF cannon in each wing. Total production of the E-3 was 1,267 units, including eighty-three for export. The E-3 in turn gave way to the Bf 109E-4 on the production line; this variant featured the modified 20mm FF/M cannon, which fired the new Minengeschoss explosive shell. The cockpit canopy was also revised to provide a square-cut design which improved pilot visibility and was also easier to produce. Many E-3s were upgraded to E-4 standard, and a fighter-bomber version was produced. It carried much the same weapons load as the E-1/B and was designated E-4/B or E-4/BN, depending on whether it was fitted with the DB 601Aa or DB 601N engine. The latter powerplant, designed for high-altitude operation, produced 1,159hp. Production of new-build Bf 109E-4s came to 496, comprising 250 E-4s, 211 E-4/Bs, fifteen E-4/Ns and twenty E-4/BNs. A further sixty-five aircraft were conversions.

The Bf 109 E-5 and E-6 were both reconnaissance variants, with a camera installation behind the cockpit. The E-5 was the reconnaissance version of the E-3, while the E-6 was a reconnaissance variant of the E-4/N. Twenty-nine E-5s and nine E-6s were built.

The next major production version was the Bf 109E-7, which was able to carry a 300l drop tank, increasing the type's range from 660km (410 miles) to a much healthier 1,325km (820 miles). A 227kg (500lb) bomb could be carried as an alternative. The E-7/U2 was a heavily armoured fighter-bomber variant, and the E-7/Z had GM-1 nitrous oxide injection system. Early E-7s were fitted with the 1,100hp DB 601A or 1,175hp DB601Aa engine, while late production aircraft, designated E-7/N, were powered by the similarly rated DB601N. Production of the Bf 109E-7 (all variants) reached 438 examples. The next sub-variant, the BF 109E-8, was basically a long-range version of the E-1 featuring a drop tank and was powered by a 1,300hp DB601E engine, while the E-9 was another reconnaissance variant, equipped with an Rb 50/30 or two Rb 32/7 cameras.

One interesting development applied to the early production Bf 109s was the Bf 109T, the T denoting *Träger* (Carrier), a variant intended for deployment on Germany's proposed aircraft carrier, the 23,200-ton *Graf Zeppelin.* Six early-model Bf 109s (B and C) and one Bf 109E were modified as trial aircraft for the carrier version, being fitted with catapult attachment points and an arrester hook. The wingspan was increased slightly to 11.08m (36ft 4in). The chord of the ailerons and slats was increased, as was the flap traverse. There was no provision for folding wings. The conversion work was carried out by Fieseler at Kassel, who received a contract to build seventy Bf 109T-1s, but after only ten examples had been produced. Work on the *Graf Zeppelin* was suspended and the remaining sixty aircraft of the order were de-navalized and completed as T-2s. Powered by a DB 601N engine, the Bf 109T-2 was armed with two 7.92mm MG 17 guns above the engine and one MG FF/M in each wing.

Late in 1939 Messerschmitt and his team, recognizing the development potential of the Bf 109, set about refining the design by taking two Bf 109E-1 airframes (V21 and V22) and fitting them with an improved engine, the DB 601E. The end result was the finest of all the Bf 109 variants, the Bf 109F 'Friedrich'.

A Messerschmitt Bf 109E-3 fighter being tested in a wind tunnel at the Luftfahrtforschungsanstalt Hermann Göring Aerial Weapon Establishment, one of the leading centres for top-secret aeronautical research, which was on the outskirts of Braunschweig, c. 1940. (Bundesarchiv)

This Bf 109D-1, bearing the fuselage code CI+58, is thought to have been one of several aircraft used as a test bed for the Daimler-Benz DB 600 engine, originally intended for the Bf 109E. This example came to grief against a railway embankment following an engine failure.

The Bf 109's narrow-track undercarriage resulted in many landing accidents. This Bf 109E bears the factory code letters BE+CF.

This interesting image clearly shows the nose-mounted armament layout of the Bf 109. The aircraft in this case is a Bf 109F-4.

The wing planform of the E-1 was retained but the overall span was reduced by two feet (61cm), a measure intended to increase the fighter's rate of roll at medium and low altitude, but this was found to have an adverse effect on the aircraft's handling, so another E-1 (V23) was fitted with new rounded (semi-elliptical) wingtips. These were also fitted to a fourth aircraft (V24, Werknummer 5604, factory code VK+AB), which also featured a modified air intake and a deeper oil-cooler bath under the engine cowling, which was redesigned to be smoother and more rounded so that the propeller spinner, adapted from that fitted to the new twin-engine Messerschmitt Me 210, blended into it smoothly. The tail unit underwent some redesign, the tailplane being moved to a new position, slightly lower and forward than its position on the Bf 109E, and the conspicuous bracing struts were deleted. A semi-retractable tailwheel was fitted and the main undercarriage legs were raked forward by 6° to improve ground handling.

Thanks to the improved aerodynamics, the more fuel-efficient DB 601E and the introduction of light-alloy drop tanks, the Bf 109F's range was increased to 1,700km (1,060 miles), compared to the Bf 109E's maximum range of 1,200km (746 miles).

Bf 109F Sub-variants

Bf 109F-1. The first to be fitted with the 1,159hp DB 601N engine driving a VDM 9-11207 propeller. Fitted with a 20mm MG FF/M Motorkanone with sixty rounds, firing through the engine hub, and two synchronized engine-mounted 7.92mm machine guns. Production was 208 aircraft, built between August 1940 and February 1941 by Messerschmitt Regensburg and the Wiener Neustädter Flugzeugwerke (WNF). The early production F-1s suffered a series of accidents in which the entire tail section was torn off. After an exhaustive investigation, it was discovered that when the bracing struts that were a feature of the Bf 109E were deleted on the Bf 109F, the rigidity of the whole tail unit was compromised, resulting in a frequency of oscillation which at certain rpm was overlapped by engine vibration. The problem was cured by reinforcing the tail section.

The Bf 109F-2 introduced the Mauser MG 151 Motorkanone with 200 rounds, supplemented by two synchronized engine-mounted 7.92mm MG 17 machine guns with 500 rounds per gun. Production of the F-2, which was shared by AGO, Arado, Erla, Messerschmitt Regensburg and WNF, ran to 1,380 aircraft. No tropicalized version of the F-2 was built, but individual aircraft were retrofitted with sand filters for service in North Africa and were known as F-2/Trop. The F-2/Z was to have been a high-altitude interceptor with GM-1 boost, but was cancelled.

Bf 109F-3. This sub-variant was fitted with the 1332hp DB 601E engine, which had broader propeller blades to improve altitude performance. Armament was the same as that of the F-1. Only fifteen examples of the F-3 were produced before production gave way to the F-4.

Bf 109F-4. Production of the F-4, armed with the new 20mm Mauser MG 151/20, reached a total of 1,841 aircraft. The type was first issued to first-line units in June 1941. Some late production aircraft were armed with two 20mm MG 151/20 cannon in faired underwing gondolas, with 135 rounds per gun, and were designated F-4/R1. Production was 240 aircraft, all built by WNF in the first three months of 1942. A high-altitude interceptor variant, with GM-1 boost and designated F-4/Z, saw extensive use; 544 examples were built,

A Bf 109F-3 of JG 3 flown by Oberfeldwebel Eberhard von Boremski, an ace with 104 victories. He survived the war only to die in a flying accident in 1963.

also in the first quarter of 1942. Finally, the Erla factory produced 576 examples of the tropicalized F-4 (trop) in the first half of 1942. A reconnaissance version of the F-4, the F-5, was proposed, but only one example was built. The Bf 109F-4/B was fitted with an under-fuselage rack to carry a 250kg (550lb) SC 250 bomb. Many experimental versions of the Bf 109F were produced, including one (c/n 14003) with a butterfly tail, another with a BMW 801 radial engine for comparative trials with the Focke-Wulf Fw 190, one with boundary layer fences in place of the leading edge slats, and one with a tricycle undercarriage for trials in connection with the Me 262 jet fighter development programme.

Bf 109G 'Gustav'

The next – and numerically the most important – production version was the Bf 109G, known as the Gustav, which was basically an F-series airframe fitted with a new 1475hp DB 605A engine. The pre-production batch of twelve Bf 109G-0 fighters retained the DB 601E engine of the Bf 109F, but when the DB 605A became available for installation in the production Bf 109G-1 the performance advantage immediately became apparent, as the new engine had the benefit of the GM 1 power-boost system, in which nitrous oxide was injected into the cylinders to boost power above the engine's rated altitude. When mixed with 100 octane fuel, the combination increased the amount of combustible mixture per unit volume of the cylinder, the increase in thermal efficiency boosting the available power for short periods. The Bf 109G-1 was armed with a single engine-mounted MG 151 cannon and two 7.9mm machine guns, but a tropicalized version, the Bf 109G-1/Trop, had two 13mm MG 131 machine

Bf 109F-1 (Werknummer 5628) of JG 51 flown by Werner Mölders, early 1941.

Bf 109F-2 of Stab./JG 53 pictured on the Eastern Front, 1941.

Bf 109F-4 'White 5' Christl flown by Oberleutnant Gerhard Barkhorn of JG 52, the second most successful air ace of all time with 301 victories, mostly over the Eastern Front.

Messerschmitt Bf 109G-2/Trop 'Black 6' on display in the Royal Air Force Museum, Hendon.

A Messerschmitt Bf 109G-6 of JG 1, seen here landing in Italy in 1944. The G-6 was the most important of the G-series.

guns mounted over the engine, two fairings being added over the gun breeches to accommodate these larger weapons.

The Bf 109G-2 was generally similar to the G-1 but had no cockpit pressurization, being used mainly in the medium- and low-level fighter reconnaissance role. The G-3 was similar to the G-1 except for its radio equipment, the FuG 7A being replaced by the FuG 16Z. The Bf 109G-4 was an unpressurized version of the G-3.

The Bf 109G-5, which was pressurized, carried a standard armament of two MG 131 and a single MG 151 and was powered by a DB 605D engine with a larger supercharger and methanol-water injection, boosting power at sea level to 1800hp. The methanol and water were carried in a jettisonable under-fuselage tank. Production of the Bf 109G-5 ran to 475 units between May 1943 and August 1944 and sub-variants included the G-5/U2 high-altitude fighter with GM-1 boost, the G-5/U2/R2 high-altitude reconnaissance fighter with GM-1 boost, and the G-5/AS high-altitude fighter with the DB 605AS engine.

The most important of all the G-series was the Bf 109G-6, which could be powered by a variety of DB 605 engine models. The G-6 was armed with two MG 131 machine guns, a single Mk 108 cannon firing through the spinner, and two MG 151/20 weapons mounted in underwing gondolas. This powerful armament was almost ideal for bomber interception, but severely reduced the aircraft's efficiency in fighter-versus-fighter combat. The Bf 109G-6/U4 carried two underwing Mk 108 cannon instead of the MG 151s.

Further sub-variants of the G-6 were the G-6/R1 fighter-bomber, which had provision for a single 550lb or 1,000lb bomb under the fuselage; the G-6/R2 which was fitted with two WGr Dödel rocket tubes in place of the underwing gondolas, each holding a 21cm missile; the G-6/U4N night fighter, fitted with FuG Naxos homing radar; the G-7, which was intended to incorporate all the refinements of the earlier models, but which never went into production; the G-8 was a fast reconnaissance fighter equipped with an Rb 12.5/7 or Rb 32/7 camera, but without the engine-mounted 30mm cannon.

Production now jumped to the Bf 109G-10, the fastest of the sub-series, which

A Bf 109G-10 with modified cockpit hood and taller, wooden tailfin.

Cockpit interior of the Bf 109G-10.

The Bf 109G-12 two-seat trainer.

A Bf 109G-6 fitted with underwing rocket tubes.

could attain 690kph (428mph) at 7,500m (24,607ft) under the power of its DB 605G engine, which had MW-50 water-methanol injection. It was armed with one Mk 108 cannon and two Mk 131 machine guns. A sub-variant, the Bf 109G-10/U4M, carried two Mk 108 cannon with eighty rounds per gun in an under-fuselage tray, but this was not very successful and was soon replaced by a fixed long-range fuel tank. The Bf 109G-10/R2 and R6 featured a new enlarged, wooden tail assembly and lengthened tailwheel leg; they were also fitted with a modified cockpit canopy known as the 'Galland Hood', which eliminated much of the cockpit frame and provided the pilot with improved visibility.

The Bf 109G-12 was a tandem two-seat trainer version, adapted from the G-1, while the G-14 was a fighter-bomber similar to the G-6, armed with an MG 151/20 cannon firing through the spinner and two MG 131 machine guns. Two more MG 151/20s or two WGr 21 rocket tubes could be carried under the wing, and the aircraft usually carried an ETC 250 bomb rack. The Bf 109G-16 was fitted with extra armour for the ground attack role, but was never used operationally. By mid-1943 the fighter-bomber task had gradually been adopted by the Focke-Wulf Fw 190, leaving the Bf 109 units to undertake the defence of the Reich.

High-altitude combat between the air defence fighters and American daylight bombers was now commonplace, and the requirement for a specialized high-altitude fighter resulted in the Bf 109H, which was a converted Bf 109F with a wingspan increased by 2m (6ft 6in). A batch of Bf 109H-0 pre-production aircraft was followed by a small number of Bf 109H-1 production machines, some being assigned to the reconnaissance role. Ceiling of the Bf 109H was 13,500m (44,293ft).

There was no Bf 109I, and the suffix J was applied to the version which was to be manufactured under licence by Hispano Aviación in Spain, so the next production version after the G-series was the Bf 109K, which was similar to the G-model with minor differences. The pre-production Bf 109K-0 aircraft were converted from G-series airframes in the autumn of 1944, and were powered by the DB 605D engine with GM-1 boost. Four sub-types were produced: the K-2 and K-4 powered by the DB 605/ASCM/DCM with MW 50 injection boosting take-off power from 1,550hp to 2,000hp, the similarly-powered Bf 109K-6, and the DB 605L-powered Bf 109K-14. The K-6 was armed with two 13mm MG 131s and three 30mm Mk 103s; the K-14 carried two MG 131s and a single Mk 108.

Projects and Prototypes

Twin Wasp 109

The success of the Bf 109 at the 1937 Zurich aviation meeting encouraged Ernst Udet, heading the development office of the RLM, to pursue the idea of offering an export version of the fighter, but with a different engine. The Bf 109 V21 development aircraft (D-IFKQ, Werknummer 1770) was therefore fitted with a 1,200hp Pratt & Whitney Twin Wasp SC-G radial engine and flew at Augsburg in August 1939. Nothing is recorded about its test flights, but the aircraft was still in existence in September 1940, when it was operated by the Deutsche Versuchsanstalt für Luftfahrt (DVL) at Braunschweig-Völkenrode, where it bore the identification code KB+11. Its eventual fate is unknown.

Bf 109Z

The Bf 109Z Zwilling (Twin), of which one prototype was built late in 1942, comprised two Bf 109F airframes joined together by means of a new wing centre section and a new tailplane, both of constant chord, in much the same way as the later North American F-82 Twin Mustang. The pilot sat in the port fuselage, the cockpit in the starboard fuselage being faired over. The Z-1 interceptor version was designed to carry a very heavy armament of five Mk 108 30mm cannon, while the Z-2, a fighter-bomber variant, was to have carried up to two 100kg (220lb) bombs, its built-in armament being reduced to two 30mm Mk 108s. The Z-1 and Z-2 were to have been powered by a pair of DB 605 engines, while two more projected variants, the Z-3 and Z-4, were to have been fitted with the Junkers Jumo 213. Span of the Bf 109Z was 13.27m (43ft 6.5in) and loaded weight 6,000kg (13,200lb). The sole completed prototype was damaged in its hangar during an Allied bombing raid in 1943 and never flew.

A scale model of the Bf 109Z. The cockpit on the starboard fuselage was faired over.

Bf 109X

One Bf 109F (D-ITXP, Werknummer 5608) was fitted with a BMW 801 radial engine and was known as the Bf 109X. The airframe differed from that of the standard Bf 109F in that the forward fuselage had a wider cross-section, and the elliptical wingtips were deleted. The Bf 109X first flew on 2 September 1940, with Fritz Wendel at the controls, and despite problems with the BMW 801A engine a test programme went ahead until early 1942, when further development was abandoned.

The Bf 109X, seen here fitted with a BMW 801 radial engine. The modified cockpit canopy resembled that of the Focke-Wulf Fw 190.

Bf 109F/4V

This was a one-off aircraft fitted with a V-type or 'butterfly' tail unit. Although the aircraft was reported to have better flight characteristics than the standard Bf 109F-4, the idea was not adopted.

The Bf 109F/4V.

Me 155

In 1942, the Messerschmitt design team began work on the design of a more advanced successor to the Bf 109. Designated Me 155, the type was based on the Bf 109G airframe, but with redesigned wings, tailplane and undercarriage to make it suitable for operation from aircraft carriers, the acquisition of which was once again on the German Navy's agenda. The undercarriage had long-stroke legs and a wide track, and it was intended to equip the aircraft with an arrester hook and catapult spools. When the RLM lost interest in carrier-borne fighters Messerschmitt reworked the design to meet requirements for a fast single-seat bomber and high-altitude fighter, the latter armed with three 20mm MG 151 cannon and powered by the new DB 628 engine. Production was about to begin when Messerschmitt was ordered to transfer the project to Blohm und Voss, who undertook much redesign work. Then designated Bv 155, three prototypes were completed and flown, the first on 8 February 1945, powered by a DB 603A engine.

Me 109R / Me 209: the Aircraft that Never Existed

In the spring of 1939, the Nazi propaganda machine broke the news that an aircraft designated Messerschmitt Me 109R had set a new world air speed record of 469.22mph (755.138kph). The designation fostered the impression that the machine was a variant of the standard Messerschmitt Bf 109 fighter. In fact, the 'Me 109R' was an entirely new design, developed for the specific purpose of attacking the record. Its actual designation was Me 209 V1, and it made its first flight on 1 August 1938, bearing the registration D-INJR. A second aircraft, the Me 209 V2 (D-IWAH) flew on

4 April 1939. Two more prototypes of the Me 209 were built. One of them, the Me 209 V4, was built as a fighter, but it failed to attain its performance expectations and offered no advantage over the Bf 109. As for the original record-breaking Me 209, its airframe – minus wings and engine – was seized by the Polish Army in 1945. It now reposes in the Polish National Aircraft Museum, Krakow.

The speed record for a piston-engine aircraft set up by the Me 209 was to stand for thirty years until 16 August 1969 when it was beaten by American pilot Darryl G. Greenamyer, who achieved an average speed of 482.533mph (777kph) in a modified Grumman F8F-2 Bearcat.

Me 309

First flown in July 1942, the Me 309 was intended as a replacement for the Bf 109 and featured several innovations, including a tricycle undercarriage. However, the aircraft's performance left much to be desired and did not represent a significant advance over that of the Bf 109G, and the project was cancelled after only four prototypes had been built.

Top and left: The Me 155 airframe was based on that of the BF 109G, and underwent much redesign after the project was taken over by Blohm und Voss.

Willy Messerschmitt congratulating test pilot Fritz Wendel after his record-breaking flight in Me 209. Wendel was lucky to survive the experience.

One of the most dangerous aircraft ever designed, the Me 209 was developed for the sole purpose of capturing the World Air Speed Record.

Bf 109 in Foreign Service

Bulgaria
The Bulgarian Air Force received nineteen Bf 109E-3s and 145 Bf 109G-2s, G-6s and G-10s. Bulgaria did not take part in the invasion of the Soviet Union but did sign the Tripartite Pact, becoming a formal ally of Nazi Germany. It also declared war on Great Britain and the USA, and in 1943–44 the Bf 109s fought many air battles in which they destroyed sixty enemy aircraft for the loss of nineteen pilots.

Croatia
The Air Force of the Independent State of Croatia (NDH) operated approximately fifty Bf 109s, including E-4s, F-2s, G-6s, G-10s and Ks, mostly delivered in 1944–45.

Czechoslovakia
During the Second World War some Bf 109 production was undertaken by the Czech Avia factory, and after hostilities had ended Avia continued to produce the Bf 109G-14 under the designation S-199. The fighter was powered by a Junkers Jumo 211F engine, the DB 605 being no longer available. Some 550 S-199s were built between 1947 and 1949.

Finland
The Finnish Air Force ordered forty-eight Bf 109G-2s, 111 G-6s and three G-8s and took delivery of 159 in total, three aircraft having been written off in transit. The Bf 109 replaced the Brewster Buffalo as the primary first-line fighter of the Finnish Air Force in 1943.

Hungary
The Royal Hungarian Air Force received three Bf 109D-1s, fifty E-3s and E-4s, sixty-six F-4s and 490 G-series aircraft. These served mainly in an air brigade attached to the Luftwaffe's VIII Fliegerkorps from the summer of 1942.

Israel
The Israeli Air Force purchased twenty-five Avia S-199 fighters from Czechoslovakia in 1948. The first examples arrived in Israel on 20 May 1948 and were used to form the Israeli Air Force's first combat unit, No

The Me 309, the unsuccessful planned replacement for the Bf 109.

A Bulgarian Air Force Bf 109G-10 being manhandled out of the mud by some soldiers.

A Bf 109G-14 of the Croatian Air Force pictured over mountainous terrain.

101 Squadron. On 28 May they went into action against Egyptian ground forces, and on 3 June the type scored its first air combat victories when Lt Modi Alon shot down two Egyptian C-47s that had just bombed Tel Aviv. The S-199s shot down six more aircraft before they were retired in October 1948.

Italy

The Regia Aeronautica purchased a single Bf 109B-2 in 1941 and used it for fast liaison. In the first half of 1943, 225 Bf 109Gs were issued to Italian fighter squadrons. Following the Italian armistice of September 1943, the Fascist Aeronautica Nazionale Repubblicana (ANR) operated 300 Bf 109Gs, two G-12s and three K-4s.

The Avia S-199 was a heavy and dangerous aircraft to fly and was dubbed '*Mezek*' (Mule) by its pilots. Here it is shown in Czech Air Force markings.

A Bf 109G-2 of the Finnish Air Force, 1943.

An Avia S-199 in the markings of the Israeli Air Force.

A Hungarian Bf 109 being rescued from the Russian snow in 1942.

A Bf 109G-2 of the ANR in northern Italy, 1943.

One of the Bf 109Es sent to Japan for evaluation by the Imperial Japanese Army Air Force in 1941.

Japan

Five Bf 109E-7s were delivered to Japan in 1941 and were extensively tested. The Allied code-name 'Mike' was later allocated to the Bf 109 when intelligence reports erroneously indicated that the type had entered service with the Imperial Japanese Army Air Force. The fighter misidentified by US intelligence was in fact the Kawasaki Ki-61, which was powered by a licence-built DB 601A engine.

Romania

The Royal Romanian Air Force (Aeronautica Regala Romana AAR) eventually operated fifty Bf 109E-3s and -4s, nineteen E-7s, two F-2s, five F-4s and at least 235 G-series fighters from German production, plus seventy-five Bf 109G-6s built by Romanian Aircraft Industries (IAR). Initial Bf 109E-3 deliveries were assigned to the 57th Squadron of Grupul 7 Vanatoare (7th Fighter Group) which was formed on 1 June 1940; the group's other squadron, the 53rd, was armed with twelve Hawker Hurricanes, delivered in 1939. Late in 1940 the 53rd Fighter Squadron and its Hurricanes were assigned to the 5th Fighter Group and more Bf 109E-3s were delivered, enabling two new squadrons (the 56th and 58th) to be formed. All fifty Bf 109Es had been delivered by the end of February 1941, the Romanian pilots having been trained during the winter by German instructors at Pipera, near Bucharest. The Luftwaffe personnel belonged to a newly formed Gruppe, I/JG 28, which was established in Romania and which became III/JG 52 in the summer of 1941, after its training task was completed. The Romanian fighters – which also included Heinkel He 112s – operated alongside their German counterparts with considerable success, the 7th Fighter group receiving fifteen ex-Luftwaffe Bf 109E-7s in 1942 as replacement aircraft.

Slovak Republic

The Slovak Air Arm operated sixteen Bf 109E-3s, fourteen E-7s and thirty G-6s.

Spain

The Spanish Air Force operated some D-1s, E-3s and 15 F-4s, and may have received several older B-types. Volunteers of Escuadrilla Azul (Blue Squadron), a Spanish volunteer unit on the Eastern Front operated the Bf 109E-4, E-7, E-7/B, F-2, F-4 (under the command of Luftflotte 2 until April 1943) and also the G-4 and G-6 (under the command of Luftflotte 4

A Messerschmitt Bf 109G-2 of the 7th Fighter Group, Romanian Air Force, 1942.

A trio of Slovak Bf 109E-4/Bs attached to JG 52, 1942.

A Bf 109F-4 of the Escuadrilla Azul on the Eastern Front. The aircraft bears the Spanish fascist insignia depicting yoke, arrows and Gordian knot.

until June 1944). A variant with a Rolls-Royce Merlin engine, the Hispano Aviación HA-1112, was produced until 1958.

Switzerland

The Swiss Air Force took delivery of the first of its 115 Bf 109s in 1938 when ten Bf 109Ds were delivered. After this, eighty 109 E-3s were purchased which were delivered from April 1939 until just before the German invasion of France in May 1940. During the war, a further four 109s (two Fs and two Gs) were acquired by the Swiss Air Force through internment. The 109Es were supplemented by eight aircraft, licence-assembled from spare parts by Doflug at

Altenrhein, delivered in 1944. Twelve Bf 109G-6s were also acquired in 1944.

Yugoslavia

The Royal Yugoslav Air Force purchased seventy-three Bf 109Es prior to the German invasion of 1941, most being assigned to the 31st and 32nd Fighter Groups. The majority of these were destroyed on the ground during the invasion. Later, Yugoslavia received about 120 Bf 109G and K variants from Bulgaria to help equip the postwar Yugoslav Air Force. The survivors were withdrawn in 1954.

One of the last HA-1112-M1L Buchóns, repainted to represent a German Bf 109, with Luftwaffe markings.

A Swiss Air Force Bf 109E-3 over the Alps. The aircraft bears underwing red and white 'neutrality' markings.

This image depicts a formation of Bf 109Gs and Ks in the camouflage and markings of the early postwar Yugoslav Air Force.

Into Service and Into Action

A Bf 109E-1 of 6./JG 234 (Schlageter), soon to be redesignated JG 26.

The first Luftwaffe unit to equip with the Bf 109 was I/JG 132 'Richthofen' at Döberitz-Elsgrund. In February 1937 it received the first of twenty-five Bf 109B-1s, replacing its Heinkel 51 fighter biplanes. Other units that armed with the Bf 109B and C were I/JG 131 at Jesau, JG 134 'Horst Wessel' at Dortmund, JG 135 at Bad Aibling, JG 136, I/JG 137 at Pardubitz, I/JG 232 'Lörzer' at Bernburg, JG 234 'Schlageter' at Cologne, and Küsten-Jägergruppe 136 on the island of Sylt. In 1939 all these units received new designations, and some of them new equipment. For example, JG 132 became JG 2 'Richthofen', while JG 134 became Zerstörergeschwader 26 (ZG 26), rearming with the twin-engined Messerschmitt Bf 110 just before the outbreak of the Second World War. In September 1938 the Luftwaffe Jagdverband (Fighter Arm) had 171 Bf 109s in service, the majority still 109B and 109C sub-variants. A year later, such was the progress of German rearmament, the figure had risen to 1,060, almost all of which were Bf 109Es.

Spanish Civil War

By the end of 1938 the Bf 109 had already proved its worth in action, having served with the German Condor Legion in the Spanish Civil War. The Messerschmitt 109 V4 prototype was sent to Spain for evaluation in December 1936 and was soon joined by two other prototypes, the V5 and V6, the three aircraft undergoing operational trials at Tablada, Seville. Combat evaluation of these prototypes proved satisfactory, and in March 1937 I and II/Jagdgruppe J.88, commanded by Leutnant Gunther Lützow, received the first of an eventual twenty-four Bf 109B-2s, with two-blade metal variable-pitch propellers. The first combat success for the Bf 109B came on 6 April 1937, when Lützow shot down a Polikarpov I-15. Apart from the latter, the main Russian-built fighter encountered by the Bf 109 in Spain was the Polikarpov I-16, which in the hands of a capable pilot could be a match for its German opponent.

Although all models of the Bf 109 then in production were evaluated in Spain, the principal variant used throughout most of the Condor Legion's involvement was the Bf 109B-2. According to the archives of the Air Chief of Staff, at the end of 1938 thirty-seven Bf 109s were in service, thirty-two based at La Cenia and five at Léon. At the end of March 1939 forty Bf 109Es were acquired and entered service alongside thirteen Heinkel He 112s. In all, ninety-six Bf 109s of all variants were deployed to Spain during the conflict.

Poland

Of the twelve Bf 109-equipped *jagdgeschwader*, seven (JG 1, JG 21, JG 26, JG 51, JG 54, JG 71 and JG 77) took part in the invasion of Poland on September 1939. Four more (JG 2, JG 3, JG 20 and JG 53) were retained for the air defence of Germany, mainly in the Berlin area, while the fifth (JG 76) was assigned to the air defence

Leutnant Werner Mölders, who was the main architect of the air combat tactics developed by the Luftwaffe in Spain, beside his Bf 109D 'Luchs' (Lynx).

A Bf 109 of Jagdgruppe J.88 carrying out an engine test.

The Bf 109 fought in Spain alongside its production rival, the Heinkel He 112.

Bf 109C-2s of I/JG 137, Bemberg, at the start of the Polish campaign.

A Bf 109D-2 of JG 52 after a forced landing during the Polish campaign.

A PZL P.11c fighter on display at the Polish Military Museum, Warsaw.

of Vienna, Austria. Some of these units were now operating the Bf 109E. The Bf 109 *geschwader* assigned to the invasion of Poland deployed 339 aircraft in total, dividing their commitment between bomber escort and ground attack. The Bf 109's main fighter opponent was the PZL P.11c, which was greatly inferior to the German aircraft.

The campaign in Poland was virtually decided by 8 September, with the Wehrmacht at the gate of Warsaw and the Polish Air Force in a desperate situation through combat attrition and a critical shortage of fuel and lack of spare parts. From 12 September the Luftwaffe began withdrawing the Bf 109s back to Germany in readiness for possible future operations in the west, leaving the Bf 110 to maintain air supremacy in Polish skies until the final collapse on 5 October. One possible reason for the early withdrawal of the Bf 109 units was the type's attrition rate: the Polish campaign had cost the Luftwaffe sixty-seven Bf 109s, a higher loss than any other German type engaged in the conflict.

Phoney War

Despite the nickname 'Phoney War' bestowed on the period from September 1939 to May 1940 because of inactivity on the Western Front, there was a great deal of activity in the air as fighters on both sides made increasing contact with each other, usually as they strove to protect reconnaissance aircraft, and it soon became apparent that the combat tactics developed during the Spanish Civil War now gave the Luftwaffe's fighter pilots a huge advantage over their opponents. Early in 1940 the Germans became increasingly aggressive, with mixed formations of Bf 109s and Bf 110s carrying out sweeps into French territory as far as Metz and Nancy. The Bf 110s usually stayed at high altitude and only engaged in combat when pressed by Allied fighters. It appeared that the Jagdwaffe was experimenting with new battle formations and offensive tactics, building on the experience of Spain and Poland. It was soon clear why. On 9 April, 1940, German forces invaded Denmark and Norway.

Fighter support for the air- and seaborne landings in Norway was initially provided by the Messerschmitt Bf 110s of I/ZG 76, whose aircraft had sufficient range to operate from their northern German base at Jever, but as German forces secured key airfields, the Bf 110s deployed to Oslo-Fornebu within hours of the invasion beginning, and the swift deployment of Bf 109 units followed. On 11 April II/JG 77 deployed to Kjevik (Kristiansand). For the next month the forty Bf 109Es of JG 77's 4, 5 and 6 Staffeln provided air cover for the German invasion forces in southern Norway, while ZG 76's Bf 110s patrolled farther afield. On 5 June, fighter reinforcements arrived in the shape of II/Trägergruppe 186, also with forty Bf 109Es, which initially established itself at Gardermoen. On 11 June 6./186 moved to Vaernes, and on the 19th 4./186 deployed to Lade, near Trondheim. On 7 July 1940, by which time the Norwegian campaign was over, II/TrGr 186 was absorbed into JG 77 and renamed III/JG 77.

During the first two months of their presence in Norway the Bf 109 units destroyed thirty-three British aircraft, mostly Lockheed Hudsons and Bristol Blenheims of RAF Coastal Command.

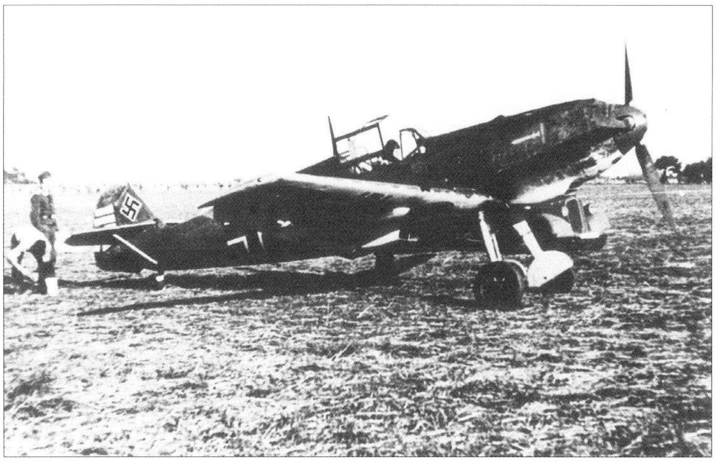

This Bf 109E, unit unknown, displays a number of victory bars on its rudder. The bars are in the form of horizontal stripes, which were soon changed to smaller vertical stripes.

Blitzkrieg

On 10 May 1940, while the fighting in Norway was still in progress, the Germans invaded France and the Low Countries. The maximum number of Bf 109Es available to the Jagdwaffe at any one time during the campaign was 860. Luftwaffe fighter operations over the Netherlands were mainly the responsibility of JG 20 and JG 26, providing cover for General Fedor von Bock's Army Group B, while JG 27 was tasked with providing a fighter umbrella over the vital bridges on the Meuse and Albert Canal, rapidly captured by the Wehrmacht. In twenty-four hours the German fighter pilots flew 340 sorties, claiming the destruction of twenty-eight Allied aircraft for the loss of only four of their own number. It was the pilots of JG 27 that, on 12 May, destroyed five out of six Fairey Battle light bombers of No 12 Squadron RAF and seven out of nine Blenheims of No 139 Squadron that attempted to attack the bridges.

A Messerschmitt Bf 109 of Stab/II. JG 77 in Norway, 1940.

On 14 May, the bridgeheads in the Sedan area were covered by the Bf 109s of JG 2, JG 53 and JG 77, and the Bf 110s of ZG 76. The fighter pilots had a field day: I/JG 53 alone claimed thirty-nine victories in the course of the day. In all the German fighters flew 814 sorties on 14 May, claiming the destruction of eighty-nine Allied aircraft. Between them, the fighters and deadly four-barrel 20mm Flakvierling mobile anti-aircraft guns destroyed thirty-nine Fairey Battles and Bristol Blenheims of the RAF's Advanced Air Striking force, over half the total number dispatched.

The Blitzkrieg – Lightning War – really began on 13 May, when the main body of German armour burst out of the Ardennes and rolled down toward the Meuse. After that the German fighters, in particular the Bf 109s, achieved mastery of the air, and in so doing they achieved saturation of the battle area by air power. The unpalatable truth is that this could have been prevented by a powerful Allied fighter force, resolutely and correctly handled; but the Allies did not have such a force. France's principal fighter type, the Morane-Saulnier MS.406, underpowered and undergunned, was no match for the Bf 109; only the American-built Curtiss Hawk 75A and the French Dewoitine D.520 could hold their own, but the former was only available in limited numbers and the latter appeared too late in the battle to make a difference. The few squadrons of Hawker Hurricanes available to the RAF in France and Belgium fought bravely and effectively, but they were always overwhelmed by the sheer numbers of the enemy.

The Lockheed Hudson reconnaissance aircraft of RAF Coastal Command suffered severely at the hands of the Bf 109 during the Norwegian campaign.

From the air support point of view, the Panzers' headlong career towards the Channel coast created some serious problems. The Bf 109 *gruppen* supporting the German armoured thrusts had to move quickly as one airstrip after another fell into German hands. For example, I/JG 2, having begun the campaign at Kirchbirg, moved to Dockendorf on 13 May, Bastogne on 14 May, Beaulieu-en-Aronne on 18 May, Signy-le-Petit on 20 May and Cambrai on 26 May. It would move six more times before the campaign ended in late June. The immense effort behind the Luftwaffe's logistics organization, created in Spain and refined in Poland, had proved its worth.

During the evacuation of Allied forces from Dunkirk, for the first time, Bf 109 pilots began to engage significant numbers of Supermarine Spitfires, as RAF Fighter

The small Belgian Air Force was soon overwhelmed. Here, a Bf 109E-1 of JG 53 is pictured on a Belgian airstrip beside the wreckage of a Belgian Fairey Fox.

Wreckage of a Fairey Battle light bomber shot down over Belgium, May 1942. The Battles of the RAF's Advanced Air Striking Force suffered appalling casualties during attacks on the Meuse bridges.

Command committed its squadrons to covering the seaborne operation. Within a few weeks, the Bf 109s would be facing a formidable combination of Spitfire and Hurricane, ably controlled by the most advanced air defence system in the world, in the skies over southern England.

Battle over Britain

At the beginning of July 1940 the Luftwaffe had some 760 Bf 109s deployed on French airfields, grouped into two tactical fighter commands within Luftflotte 2 (460) and Luftflotte 3 (300). In June, small-scale raids on so-called 'fringe' targets such as ports around the English coast took place, and early in July the Luftwaffe began heavier attacks on shipping in the English Channel, the aim being to probe Fighter Command's defences and reaction times, in addition to inflicting physical damage on its fighter squadrons.

The air strategy adopted by Luftwaffe commander Reichsmarschall Hermann Göring seemed simple enough on paper, but proved much more difficult to implement in practice. Firstly, the RAF's fighters were to be destroyed in the air and on the ground by concentric attacks moving progressively inland, starting with attacks on airfields within a radius of ninety to sixty miles (150 to 100km) south of London. These attacks would take place over a five-day period and would be followed by a three-day assault on targets that lay between sixty and thirty miles (150 and 50km) from the capital. The assault would be completed with a five-day series of attacks on airfields situated within thirty miles of London, after which it was hoped the invasion could be launched. However, the whole plan was based on a fundamentally flawed intelligence assessment, which among other things predicted that Fighter Command's strength would rapidly decline once the intensified air

Bf 109Es of I.(J)/LG 2, the Luftwaffe's fighter-bomber *gruppe* in the Battle of France. The aircraft nearest the camera carries the so-called Spanienkreuz aft of the Balkenkreuz; this was introduced after the Polish campaign by Hauptmann Harro Harder, who had previously commanded I/J 88 in Spain. The swastika insignia has been edited out of this image.

A Messerschmitt Bf 109E-3 of JG 2 after making a forced landing during operations in France, 1940.

Luftwaffe air ace Helmut Wick climbing from the cockpit of his Bf 109E-4 of Stab.I/JG 2. Wick's score stood at fourteen confirmed victories when the Battle of France ended.

The Supermarine Spitfire fought the Bf 109 for the first time over Dunkirk. The two fighters were fairly evenly matched.

Both above: Bf 109s of JG 26 over the English Channel, August 1940.

One that didn't make it back to base: a Bf 109E in the shallows off the French coast.

If the Bf 109 had been fitted with auxiliary fuel tanks, as seen on this Bf 109G, the outcome of the Battle of Britain might have been very different.

battle had started; the excellent British aircraft repair and replacement facilities were totally disregarded. The short endurance of the Bf 109, which together with the long approach over the Channel would substantially curtail its combat time over target, was not mentioned; neither was the obvious fact that the short range of the Bf 109 would determine the range of penetration of the bombers in daylight, leaving many of the fighter airfields and industrial installations farther inland out of reach.

The problem might have been solved fairly easily had the Bf 109s been fitted with auxiliary fuel tanks, which could be jettisoned just before combat. The fact that they were not was accounted for, at least in part, by Göring's belief that the long-range task could be successfully performed by the twin-engine Messerschmitt Bf 110 Zerstörer (Destroyer), which had been a pet project of his from its inception. In practice, the Bf 110 units suffered appalling losses in combat with Fighter Command's Spitfires and Hurricanes over England, and it was the Bf 109 that was forced to bear the burden of bomber escort work. But the Bf 109E never had more than twenty minutes of combat time in which to protect its bombers, and its combat radius would take it only as far as the northern suburbs of London. Had the 109 been able to extend its time in the combat area by another thirty minutes through the use of external fuel tanks, then the consequences to Fighter Command might have been dire.

On 12 August 1940, as a prelude to the main offensive against the British Isles, attacks were made on Britain's vital radar stations by bomb-carrying Bf 109s and 110s of Erpobungsgruppe 210 (a unit originally established to evaluate the unsuccessful Me 210, hence its designation) and Junkers Ju 88s of KG 51 and KG 54. The damage was quickly repaired, and surprisingly no further attacks were carried out on these targets.

Throughout the battle, which began in earnest on 13 August, it was the Bf 109 that was the main cause of Fighter Command's losses. Of the thirty-four RAF fighters lost in the fierce dogfighting of 15 August, for example – the heaviest day of the whole battle – twenty-six were brought down by Bf 109s. In contrast, the German fighter arm, the Jagdwaffe, lost only nine Bf 109s in combat that day, although twenty-one twin-engine Bf 110s were destroyed, several in attacks on targets in northern England by the squadrons of Luftflotte 5, based in Norway and Denmark. The Luftwaffe's total loss on 15 August was seventy-one fighters and bombers. Air combat in August

Leutnant Horst Marx, a pilot with 3. Staffel Erprobungsgruppe 210, and his Bf 109 E-3/B.

Willing hands of RAF personnel, assisted by a couple of carthorses, recovering a Bf 109E-1 of 5./JG 53 from a field at Smeeth, Kent, where its last sortie came to an abrupt end. Its pilot, Leutnant Otto Zauner, an ace with ten victories, was taken prisoner.

cost the RAF 326 fighters (213 Hurricanes and 113 Spitfires), with a further forty-four and forty damaged respectively; the Luftwaffe's fighter losses were 336 (217 Bf 109s and 119 Bf 110s), with forty-five and forty damaged respectively. Fighter Command suffered 130 pilots killed, with 106 more wounded; Luftwaffe fighter aircrew losses amounted to 134, of which the crews of the Bf 110s accounted for eighty. Another 113 Luftwaffe aircrew were wounded.

By this time the deadline for the establishment of Luftwaffe air superiority over the planned invasion areas of southern England had passed. Indeed, the Germans never came close to achieving it, mainly because they never had enough single-engine fighters to do so. Also, the *jagdgeschwader* were hampered throughout the battle by faulty intelligence, by a move away from attacks on the RAF's fighter airfields, and by Hermann Göring's directive that the fighters were to provide close escort to the bombers, so robbing them of a vital tactical advantage.

On 17 September, two days after the Luftwaffe suffered particularly heavy losses on a massed attack on London, Hitler postponed the planned invasion of Britain. The beginning of October 1940 saw a change in the Luftwaffe's tactics. Attacks on London and targets in southern England were now made by formations of bomb-carrying Messerschmitts operating at high level. At Göring's instigation, one *staffel* of each Bf 109 *geschwade*r in the Channel coast area now rearmed with either Bf 109E-1/B or Bf 109E-7 and E-8 fighter-bombers, concentrating their efforts on London. The daylight offensive against Britain was at an end, but the ordeal of Britain's cities by night was just beginning.

Balkan Campaign

Because of the Bf 109F's structural problems, which delayed the variant's entry into full operational service until May 1941,

The artwork on this Bf 109E of III/JG 54 'Grünherz' depicts a hunter with a brace of Spitfires hanging from his belt. Having enjoyed much success during the Battle of Britain, JG 54 rearmed with the Bf 109F and was transferred to the Eastern Front.

This Bf 109E-1 of 7./JG 27 overturned when its pilot, Oberleutnant Karl Fischer, tried to make a forced landing in Windsor Great Park after sustaining battle damage in combat with RAF fighters.

This Bf 109E of I/JG 2 'Richthofen' was disabled by RAF fighters during an attack on Shoreham airfield on 13 August 1940. Its pilot, Oberleutnant Paul Temme, made a successful belly landing and was taken prisoner.

The Bf 109F was evaluated in the later stage of the Battle of Britain by Luftwaffe ace and supreme tactician Werner Mölders, but structural problems delayed its full operational debut.

A Bf 109E-3 of Stab.III/JG 27 at Kozani, Greece, April 1941.

the Bf 109E remained the mainstay of the Jagdwaffe's single-engine fighter force during the Wehrmacht's invasion of Yugoslaviaia and Greece in April/May that year. The invasion of Yugoslavia, launched on 6 April, was supported by Jagdgeschwader 27, 54 and 77, their Bf 109Es operating from airfields in Austria, Romania and Bulgaria. The Yugoslav Air Force's Bf 109s, already suffering from a shortage of spare parts, were soon overwhelmed, the majority being destroyed on the ground. The simultaneous invasion of Greece, also launched on 6 April, was mainly supported by JG 27, protecting the Ju 87 Stukas of VIII Fliegerkorps operating from their Bulgarian bases. As the campaign in Greece progressed and airfields were captured, II/ and III/JG 27 moved forward with the Stukas, just as they had done during the Battle of France, and by 26 April their Bf 109s were established at Eleusis, near Athens. They remained there on air-defence duties for some weeks after the close of the Greek campaign before returning to the Reich in June. Meanwhile, the Bf 109 formations on Luftflotte IV's order of battle – II./ and III./ JG 77, III./JG 52 and I.(J)LG 2 – had been assigned to cover the airborne assault on the island of Crete in May, after which they withdrew to their airfields in Romania to rearm with the Bf 109F.

A Bf 109E of JG 27 at Ain-el-Gazala, 1941.

North Africa

In March 1941, detachments of I/JG 27 deployed to Sicily to participate in the air offensive against Malta with its Bf 109E-7 fighter-bombers. In the following month the whole *gruppe* moved to Ain-el-Gazala in Libya and embarked on intensive operations in support of General Erwin Rommel's recently arrived Afrika Korps. In September, the arrival of the first Bf 109F-4/Trop fighters of II/JG 27 in North Africa enabled I Gruppe to return to Germany, one *staffel* at a time, to rearm with similar aircraft, its Bf 109E-7s being allocated to Luftwaffe units in Italy and Greece. In December 1941 III/JG 27, also armed with the Bf 109F-4/Trop – having left its Bf 109Es with other units in Russia - also deployed to North Africa, so that the whole *geschwader* was now operating in the theatre. By the end of 1941 I and II/ Gruppen JG 27 had claimed 92 victories in North Africa for the loss of 41 Bf 109s.

The principal task of JG 27 was to escort the Stuka dive-bombers of Stukageschwader 3, in which role it was involved in the fierce air battles of mid-1942. On 20 June the Luftwaffe and Regia Aeronautica launched a massive assault on the defences of Tobruk, the Germans flying 580 sorties and the Italians 177 on this one day. Tobruk fell, but the Axis forces pushed on toward Egypt with severely depleted air cover, aircraft serviceability having suffered greatly as a result of this effort and an earlier one at Bir Hakim, when the Afrika Korps outflanked the defensive line at Gazala. By this time, the Luftwaffe units were becoming desperately short of fuel and spare parts; at times. JG 27 was down to about a dozen serviceable fighters. Attacks on Rommel's Mediterranean convoys by strike aircraft and submarines based on the strategically vital island of Malta were taking a severe toll.

The Luftwaffe's involvement in the air offensive against Malta had begun in January 1941, this initial phase lasting until March, when the German units were withdrawn from Sicily in March 1941 to take part in the Balkans campaign and later

A Bf 109F-4/Trop of JG 27 preparing for takeoff. The mechanic walking away is carrying the engine starting tool.

JG 27's main task was to provide protection for the vulnerable Junkers Ju 87 dive-bomber, which – like this one – was also used by the Regia Aeronautica. The biplane in the background is a Fiat CR.42 fighter.

the invasion of Russia, leaving the Regia Aeronautica to continue the air offensive against Malta. The Luftwaffe returned to Sicily in strength toward the end of the year, its bomber force now comprising the Junkers Ju 88s of Fliegerkorps II, and this time it had considerable fighter support. In January 1942 all three *gruppen* of JG 53 were established on the Sicilian airfields, I Gruppe being armed with the Bf 109F-4 and the other two with the Bf 109F-4/Z

Hans-Joachim Marseille, leading ace of the desert war, climbing into the cockpit of his Bf 109F-4 'Yellow 14'.

A Bf 109F-2/Trop of JG 77, abandoned and captured by Australian forces in Libya, 1942.

fighter-bomber. In May 1942, I/JG 53 redeployed to the Russian Front, and in June the other two redeployed respectively to Pantelleria and North Africa; II/JG 53 began to receive the Bf 109G-4 in August, and III/JG 53 also began to re-equip in November. Elements of III/JG 3 also operated over Malta in January and February 1942.

In October 1942 Malta suffered a further fierce onslaught by Luftwaffe units redeployed from Russia. It lasted seventeen days, with heavy losses on both sides, and ended when the offensive was called off by Field Marshal Albert Kesselring, commanding Luftflotte 2 in Sicily. The British offensive at El Alamein was now in progress, and all available German air power in the Mediterranean theatre was assigned to the support of the Afrika Korps.

In North Africa, the morale of the fighter pilots of JG 27, already at a low ebb through a combination of combat losses, battle fatigue and aircraft availability problems, suffered a further blow with the death of the *geschwader*'s leading air ace, Leutnant Hans-Joachim Marseille. In September 1942, Marseille's tally of enemy aircraft destroyed rose to 158, but on 30 September, returning to his base after an escort mission, his Bf 109F suffered engine trouble and he was compelled to bale out of a cockpit filled with smoke. His body struck the tailplane and he fell to his death, his parachute failing to open.

In December 1942, the whole of JG 27 was withdrawn from the North African theatre and redeployed to Sicily before being re-assigned to the defence of the Reich in 1943. Its place was taken by JG 77, which now had the task of covering the retreat of the Axis forces into Tunisia. It, too, departed in April 1943, withdrawing to bases in Sicily, Italy and the Balkans. Its ground crews were left behind to join the thousands of Axis troops who surrendered in May.

A restored Polikarpov I-16 in the markings of the Spanish Republican Air Arm. The fighter was dubbed '*Mosca*' (Fly) by the Republicans and '*Rata*' (Rat) by the Nationalists.

The most numerous French fighter in 1940 was the Morane-Saulnier MS 406, a restored example of which is seen in this image.

Without doubt, the best French fighter type was the Dewoitine D.520, but its numbers were too few to influence the outcome of the air battle over France.

The Curtiss Hawk 75A performed well in French service, but was undergunned.

A Bf 109F-4 of JG 27 pictured during a deployment to Gela, Sicily, for operations over Malta in 1942.

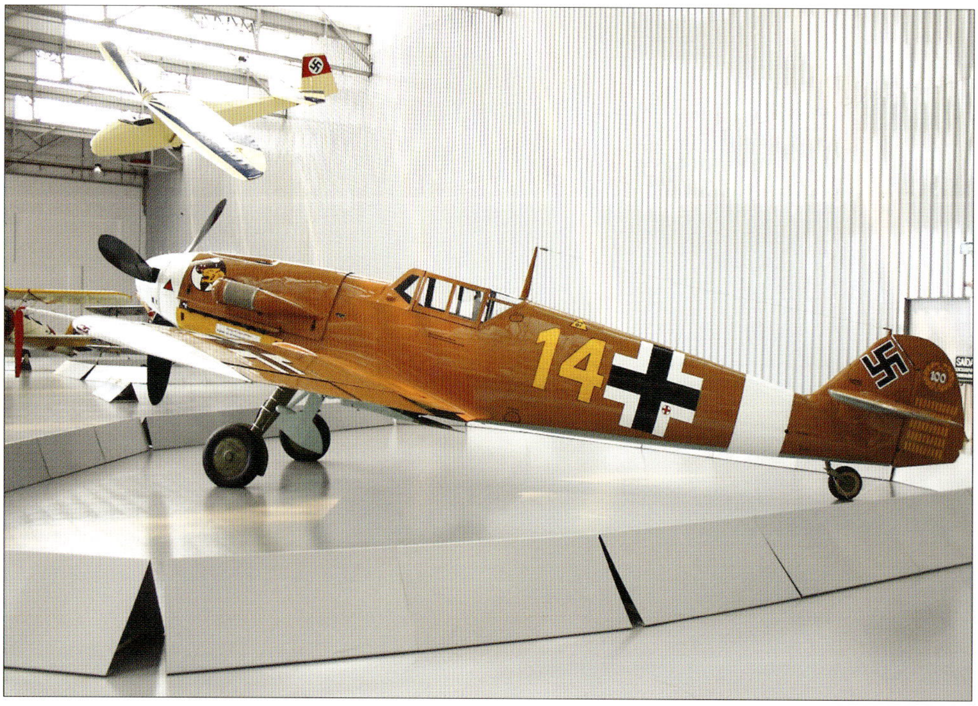

This Messerschmitt Bf 109G-2 is painted to represent the 'Yellow 14' of 3./JG 27 flown by German ace Hans-Joachim Marseille.

The Eastern Front

At dawn on 22 June 1941, the Germans launched Operation Barbarossa, the invasion of the Soviet Union. Throughout the day, Soviet airfields and other installations were subjected to heavy attacks by 510 bombers and 290 dive-bombers, supported by 440 Bf 109s and forty Bf 110s. Soviet losses in the day's operations were 1,167 aircraft destroyed on the ground and 322 in the air; the Luftwaffe's loss was thirty-five. It was the greatest victory ever achieved in a single day by one air force over another.

Most of the German single-engine fighter units were now armed with the Bf 109F. A notable exception was II (Schlachtgruppe) LG 2, which began the offensive from its base at Praszniki in Poland, near the Lithuanian border. Armed with thirty-seven Bf 109E-4/B and seventeen Henschel Hs 123 fighter-bombers, it formed part of the ground-attack support for 3 Panzergruppe, and featured in the capture of Minsk in June. Its losses were heavy, and by the end of July it was down to just fourteen serviceable aircraft.

The Soviet Air Force, although it fought desperately, was deficient in equipment and was no match for the experienced Luftwaffe units. On 24 June, for example, the Bf 109 pilots of JG 51, covering the advance of 2 Panzergruppe, destroyed eighty-one enemy aircraft, including fifty-seven Tupolev SB-2 bombers, and the next day they shot down a further eighty-three SB-2s. On that same day the Bf 109Fs of JG 54 Grünherz, supporting 4 Panzergruppe, destroyed sixty-five Russian aircraft. In September 1941 JG 54 redeployed to the Leningrad Front in support of the Ju 87 Stukas of I/St.G 2 and III/St.G 2, tasked with neutralizing the Soviet Baltic Fleet in Kronstadt. The harbour was defended by the fighters of the Baltic Fleet Air Force and the 7th Fighter Air Corps. Between them, these two Soviet formations mustered some 1,900 aircraft, of which about 1,200 – mostly obsolescent types – were directly engaged in the Leningrad sector. The Russians never came close to challenging German air superiority. Between 22 June and 5 December 1941 JG 54 claimed the destruction of 1,078 Russian aircraft for the loss of forty-six Bf 109Fs in air combat and one on the ground.

At the other end of the battlefront, while the siege of Leningrad settled down into a grim stalemate that would last over two years and cost the lives of a million civilians and 300,000 Russian soldiers, the Jagdwaffe's order of battle underwent some changes. In September, I/JG 3 was withdrawn and returned to Germany to rearm with the Bf 109F-4, and in October II/JG 3 turned over its Messerschmitts to III/JG 77 and also returned to Germany to re-form and rearm. III/JG 3 followed suit in November, handing over its Bf 109s to JG 51.

In September 1941, I/JG 52 had arrived on the Eastern Front from Holland, joining the other two *gruppen* of the *geschwader* on bases near the Volga. In October, the *geschwader*'s strength was augmented by a Croation volunteer unit, 15.(kroatische)/Jagdgeschwader 52, equipped with a mixture of Bf 109Es and -Fs, which was established at Mariupol. The remaining *jagdgeschwader* supporting Army Group South, JG 77, had suffered badly in the drive toward the Crimea, and its assets were badly depleted by the time II and III Gruppen assembled at Mariupol in December.

On 20 February 1942, Junkers Ju 52 transport aircraft launched a major airlift

A Bf 109E-4/B and Henschel 123 ground-attack biplanes

A Bf 109F of JG 54 after a forced landing on the Leningrad Front, 1941.

A Junkers Ju 52/3m transport flying into the Demyansk pocket in February 1942.

The Yakovlev Yak-9 seen here in the markings of the French 'Normandie-Niemen' Regiment, which fought alongside the Russians.

The Focke-Wulf Fw 190 replaced the Bf 109 in many Jagdwaffe units on the Eastern Front.

Oberfeldwebel Otto Wessling on the wing of his Bf 109F 'Yellow 2' of JG 3 in September 1942, at the start of the Battle of Stalingrad.

operation to an airstrip at Demyansk, south of Leningrad, to supply 100,000 troops of the German X and XI Army Corps, encircled by the Red Army's January offensive. Eight transport *gruppen* were eventually involved. At first the Ju 52s flew in singly at low level, but as losses increased due to Soviet air action, the transports adopted tight formations, with strong fighter escort provided by the Bf 109Fs of III/JG 3 and I/JG 51. The airlift was successful: up to 20 May 1942, when a land corridor to the pocket was opened, the Ju 52s flew in 24,303 tons of supplies – a daily average of 276 tons – to the Demyansk pocket. In addition, five million gallons of petrol and 15,446 replacements were flown in, and 22,093 wounded evacuated. But the Germans lost 262 Ju 52s, many as a result of accidents in the winter conditions.

The success of the Demyansk airlift, albeit at such high cost, was to have a dangerous consequence. It convinced Reichsmarschall Hermann Göring, the Luftwaffe C-in-C, that the Luftwaffe was capable of resupplying the German Sixth Army, trapped at Stalingrad in the winter of 1942/3. The promises he made were empty, and the Sixth Army went down in defeat.

The winter of 1942/43 showed that Russian fighter pilots could match, and often outfight, their German counterparts. The days when Luftwaffe aces could notch up fantastic scores against an inexperienced, poorly trained enemy were gone forever, and now, in the early weeks of 1943, Russian fighter squadrons everywhere along thee 1200-mile front were beginning to receive equipment that was more than a match for the Bf 109, and which were capable of meeting the latest Focke-Wulf Fw 190s on equal terms. As well as the Lavochkin La-5, there was the Yakovlev Yak-9, which was a progressive development of the Yak-1. A heavy fighter, the Yak-9 – which was to be built in greater numbers than any other Russian fighter – could also be used in the fighter-bomber and reconnaissance roles, and one version armed with a 37mm cannon was effective against armour.

By the start of the battle for Stalingrad, the Jagdwaffe units in Russia had re-equipped, or were in the process of re-equipping with either the Focke-Wulf Fw 190 or the improved Messerschmitt Bf 109G. The first of the Bf 109G series fighters arrived on the Eastern Front late in 1942, in time to take part in the air battles over Stalingrad. Already, the battles of 1942 had demonstrated that the Bf 109F could no longer hold its own against the latest Soviet fighter types. In August 1942, for example, JG 51 suffered heavier losses than anything previously experienced during the conflict; 101 Bf 109s were destroyed or written off from all causes during the month, with seventeen pilots killed, missing, or hospitalized. Early in September 1942, I./JG 51 was withdrawn to convert to the Focke-Wulf Fw 190.

On the Northern Front, JG 54 received the first of its Fw 190s in February 1943, and other Jagdwaffe units followed suit throughout the year. The remaining Bf 109-equipped *staffeln* fought on, and during the Battle of Kursk in August 1943 it fell to the Bf 109Gs of JG 52 to provide escort for the German ground-attack aircraft. This was to remain the pattern for the remainder of the war in the east, as the Luftwaffe battled against ever-increasing odds to face ultimate defeat.

In the Lavochkin La-5, the Russians at last had a fighter that was a match for both the Messerschmitt Bf 109 and the Focke-Wulf Fw 190.

Servicing a Bf 109 in the Crimea, 1942.

On 9 May 1945, the German garrison in Prague, the last pocket of resistance, surrendered. On that day, Guards Major Viktor Golubev, the sixteenth-ranking Soviet air ace, destroyed a Bf 109 over the city. As far as may be ascertained, this was the last aircraft destroyed in combat during the European war.

Defence of the Reich

At the outbreak of the Second World War, the air defence of northwest Germany and the German Bight area was assigned to II/ JG 77, armed with Bf 109Es, and it was this unit that first made contact with the bombers of the Royal Air Force, which launched its first attacks on German targets – restricted to units of the German Navy for the time being – on 4 September 1939. On that day one of II/JG 77's pilots, Unteroffizier Alfred Held, shot down a Vickers Wellington. It was the Luftwaffe's first victory against the RAF's strategic bomber force.

Further attempts to attack the German fleet in Wilhelmshaven and the Jade estuary in December cost RAF Bomber Command a further seventeen Wellingtons, leading the RAF to abandon daylight attacks and develop a night offensive, although much of its activities up to the German Blitzkrieg in May 1940 involved laying mines off the enemy coast and dropping propaganda leaflets.

In 1941, the Fw 190A series fighter began partially to replace the Bf 109 as the main Luftwaffe fighter type. The Fw 190A proved to be more manoeuvrable and better armed, but its performance above 6,100m (20,000ft) decreased and was only rectified in later models. The Bf 109 variants could fight well at high altitudes and were a match for Allied fighters in performance. It was decided by the OKL to keep both the Fw 190 and Bf 109 in production.

In April 1942 both types were committed to providing a fighter umbrella for the German battlecruisers *Scharnhorst* and *Gneisenau* and the heavy cruiser *Prinz Eugen*, which broke out of the Channel ports and headed for Germany in Operation Cerberus, better known as the 'Channel Dash'. To cover the breakout, General Adolf Galland, the General der Jagdflieger, had assembled a force of some 250 fighters, mostly Bf 109Fs, drawn from the two

Bf 109Fs of JG 1 preparing for night sortie from a Dutch airfield, 1942.

Vickers Wellington bombers of No IX Squadron, RAF Bomber Command, one of the first to engage Bf 109s off northern Germany.

B-17 Flying Fortresses en route to a target in Germany.

jagdgeschwader (JG 2 and JG 26) already in the Channel area, JG 1 in the Netherlands and Jagdfliegerschule 5 at Bernay, between Caen and Paris. All the German warships reached their home waters, although *Scharnhorst* was damaged by a mine.

In late 1941 and the first half of 1942 Bf 109F-4/B fighter-bombers of 10. (Jabo) JG 2 and 10. (Jabo) JG 26 carried out many attacks on shipping and high-value targets on the southern coast of England. Between 30 November 1941 and 26 July 1942, JG 2 claimed the destruction of twenty ships totalling 63,000 tons, while JG 26 claimed to have destroyed eight railway installations, eight barracks, six ships, five factories, two gasholders and two harbour installations. By this time the two *geschwader* had re-equipped with the Focke-Wulf Fw 190, the fighter-bomber units receiving the Fw 190A-3/U1, which could carry a 500kg (1,100lb) bomb.

On 27 January 1943, VIIIth Bomber Command of the United States Eighth Army Air Force, following a series of attacks on 'fringe' targets in France and the Low Countries, made its first raid on Germany when sixty-four B-17s and B-24s bombed Wilhelmshaven. American losses were light, which encouraged deeper-penetration raids, but a foretaste of what the Americans might expect came on 17 April when 117 B-17s attacking the Focke-Wulf aircraft factories in Bremen were subjected to determined attacks by the Bf 109s of JG 1, which shot down fifteen bombers and damaged forty-eight more.

On 17 August 1943 VIIIth Bomber Command suffered its heaviest loss to date when 376 B-17s were dispatched to attack ball-bearing factories at Schweinfurt and the Messerschmitt assembly plant at Regensburg. Both targets were hit, but sixty bombers were shot down and as many more badly damaged. During this operation the B-17s were subjected to attacks by Bf 109Gs of JG 1, JG 3, JG 26 and JG 27 armed with underwing 210mm air-to-air rockets.

Worse was to come. On 14 October VIIIth Bomber Command dispatched 291 B-17s on a second attack on the Schweinfurt ball-bearing factories. Seventy-seven bombers failed to return and 133 more were damaged. This day, known as 'Black Thursday', was the climax of a week's operations that cost the Command 148 heavy bombers and nearly 1,500 aircrew.

It was a rate of attrition that could not be sustained. The Luftwaffe had won air superiority in the daylight battle over Germany, and it would not swing back in the Allies' favour until long-range escort fighters were available in sufficient numbers. No more deep penetrations in clear weather were made into Germany for the rest of 1943, a command decision based on the lack of escort fighters, and the need for recuperating the bomber force after its losses on 14 October.

Meanwhile, the Bf 109 had also become involved in defensive operations against RAF Bomber Command's night offensive, which had been steadily growing in strength. These night operations, known as *Wilde Sau* (Wild Boar) were the brainchild of a decorated bomber pilot, Major Hajo Hermann, who suggested that single-seat fighters could operate in the bombers' general target area using the light of target indicators, massed searchlights and the fires on the ground to spot their targets. Hermann's idea led to the establishment of Jagdgeschwader 300, using Fw 190A and Bf 109G fighters. Special variants of the Bf 109 were later adapted for this night fighter duty, being the Bf 109 G-6(N) and Bf 109 G-6(Y), the former fitted with the FuG 350 Naxos Z passive homing detector and the latter with the 'Y' interception radio system; initially the single-seat fighters used no radar or radio aids.

The early weeks of 1944 saw the deployment of the fighter that would change the course of the air war in Western Europe: the North American P-51 Mustang. Not only could the P-51 escort the American daylight bombers all the way to distant targets such as Berlin and back, it could also mount effective strafing attacks on enemy airfields within the Reich territory. Its appearance forced a complete revision of the Luftwaffe's fighter defences and defensive organization. Three air divisions were assigned to defend German air space. The 1st Fighter Division protected the Netherlands and northwest Germany; the 2nd Fighter Division, based around Hamburg, was responsible for the defence of Denmark and north–central Germany; the 3rd Fighter Division, in effect the first line of defence, protected German air space along the French border, extending into Belgium and Luxembourg; the 4th Fighter Division was assigned to the defence of Berlin; and the 5th Fighter Division's task was to defend central and southern Germany. The latter area was assuming growing importance, for B-17s and B-24s of the US Fifteenth Army Air Force were now operating from airfields in Italy, from where they were well placed to attack targets that were out of reach of the British-based Eighth AAF.

The Jagdwaffe's fighter interception tactics were also revised. While heavily armed Fw 190s known as *Sturmböcke* (Battering Rams) were to engage the American bomber streams, the units equipped with the Bf 109, whose high-altitude performance was better than that of the Fw 190, would engage the escort fighters and endeavour to disperse them, two Bf 109 *gruppen* taking

B-17s over Schweinfurt, 17 August 1943.

A Messerschmitt Bf 109G-6(N) fitted with Naxos Z passive homing detector, visible behind the cockpit.

B-24s of the Fifteenth US Army Air Force attacking the Romanian oilfields at Ploesti, August 1943.

A B-24, one engine smoking, flying through a flak barrage.

P-51D Mustangs of the 361st Fighter Group, Little Walden, Essex, 1944.

Third : American troops examining a Bf 109G of JG 53 brought down during Operation Bodenplatte, 1 January 1945.

Bottom: End of days: a young American soldier poses beside the wreck of a JG 3 Bf 109K, April 1945.

off ahead of the main interception force for this purpose. Twin-engine Bf 110s armed with 210cm rockets would also attack the bomber formations in an effort to break them up. The new tactics were tried out on 6 March 1944, which saw the first USAAF raid on Berlin. The raid was costly, forty-six bombers and twenty-three fighters being lost, and a further attack on 8 March cost the Americans a further fifty-four aircraft, but the Jagdwaffe was also suffering severe attrition, losing an average of fifty fighters every time the Luftwaffe mounted a major attack. On 16 March, Mustangs of VIIIth Fighter Command destroyed twenty-six out of forty-three Bf 110s of ZG 76 which attempted to intercept B-17s attacking Augsburg, after which the Bf 110 was withdrawn from the daylight air-defence role.

In the months following the Allied landings in Normandy in June 1944 the Allies established complete air superiority in northwest Europe, despite the introduction of new and revolutionary German fighter like the Me 262 jet, whose airfields came under constant air attack. By the end of the year Luftwaffe fighter losses were very heavy, and became heavier still during Operation Bodenplatte (Baseplate), a massive attack on Allied airfields in Belgium, Holland and northern France by about 800 fighter-bombers on 1 January 1945. Although it inflicted considerable damage, the attack cost the Germans 150 day fighters, including many of its remaining Bf 109s.

There was one final act to be played out. With the war in Europe only a month away from its end, the Luftwaffe ordered the establishment of a task force known as Sonderkommando Elbe, another brainchild of Hajo Hermann. About 180 Bf 109Gs were assigned to it, drawn from fighter units everywhere. They were stripped of radios and other equipment and their armament was reduced to single nose-mounted MG 131 machine gun with sixty rounds of ammunition. Their task was to ram American bombers, the pilots supposedly baling out just before impact.

The unit's sole mission was flown on 7 April 1945, with 143 Bf 109s taking off from five airfields in Germany and one outside Prague. Only fifteen ramming attacks were actually made, resulting in the loss of eight bombers. Some fifty Bf 109s failed to return.

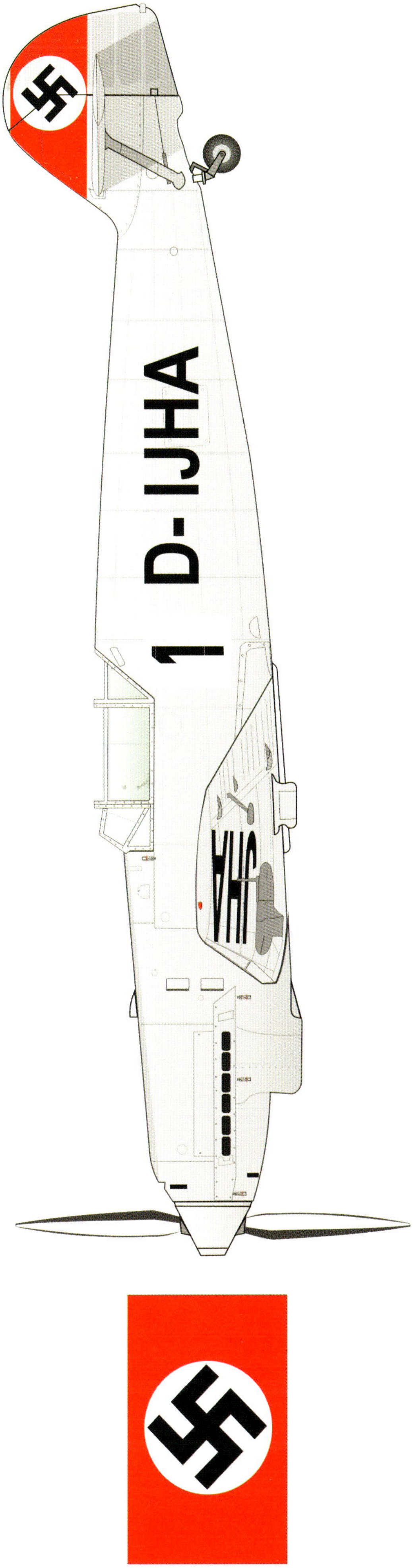

Bf 109V7 prototype/development aircraft, BFW as flown at Zürich, D-IJHA/1.

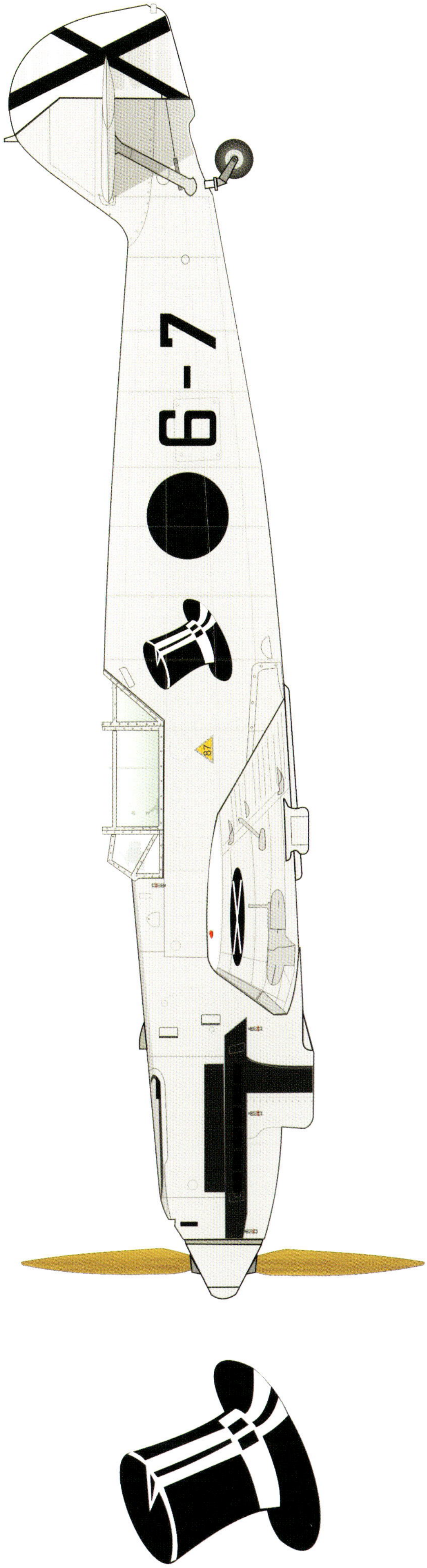

Spanish Civil War Bf 109B-1, Legion Condor, 6-7.

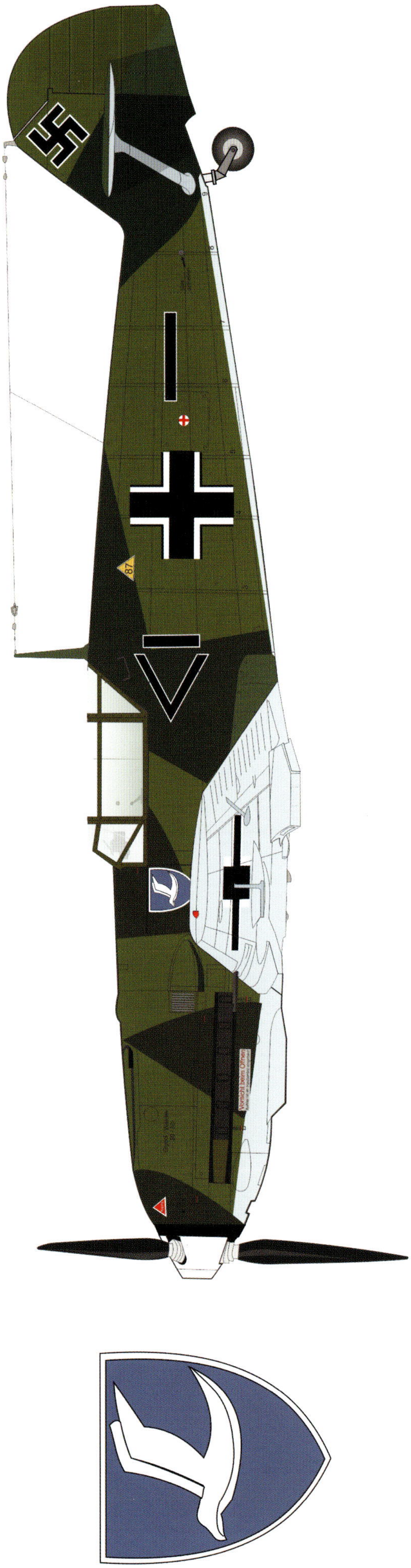

Bf 109E-3 of II./JG 77.

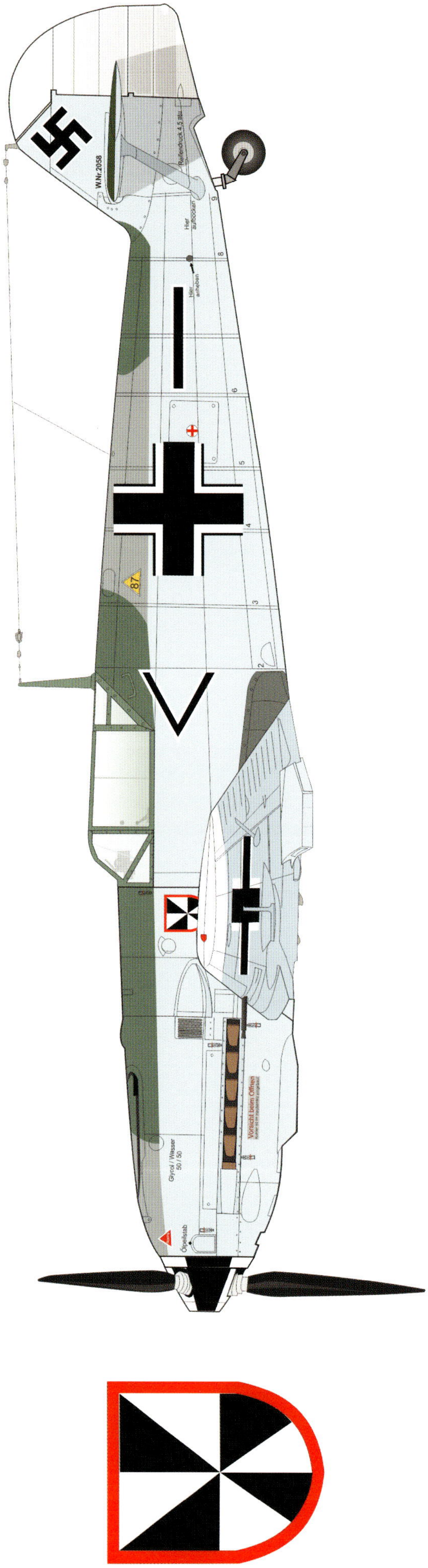

Bf 109E-4 'Black Chevron' of JG 3 flown by Franz von Werra, Battle of Britain.

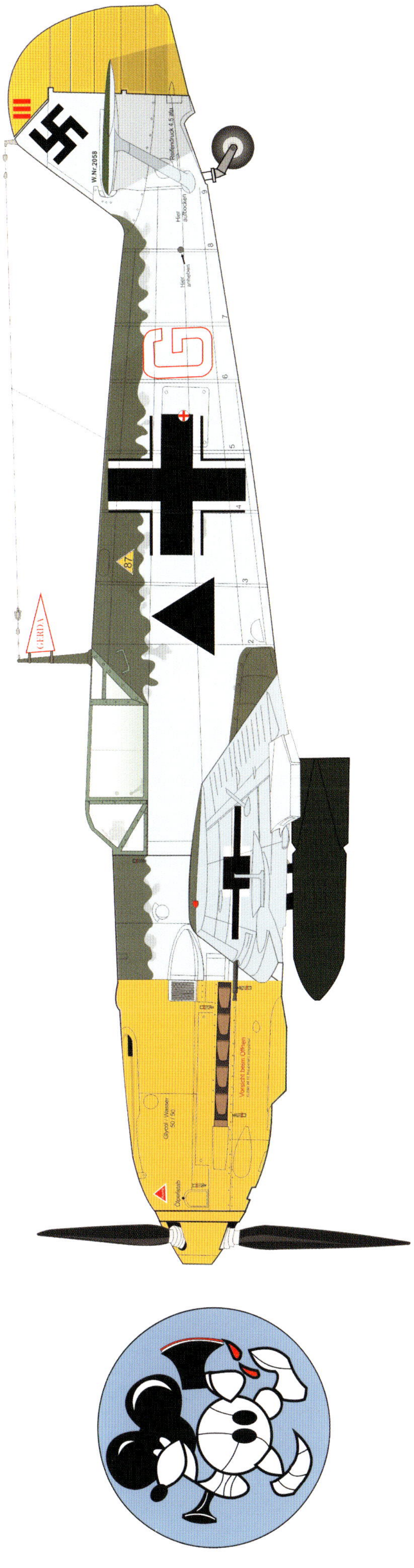

Bf 109E-1/B 'White G' of 4./LG 2 used in fighter-bomber attacks on southern England, 1940-41.

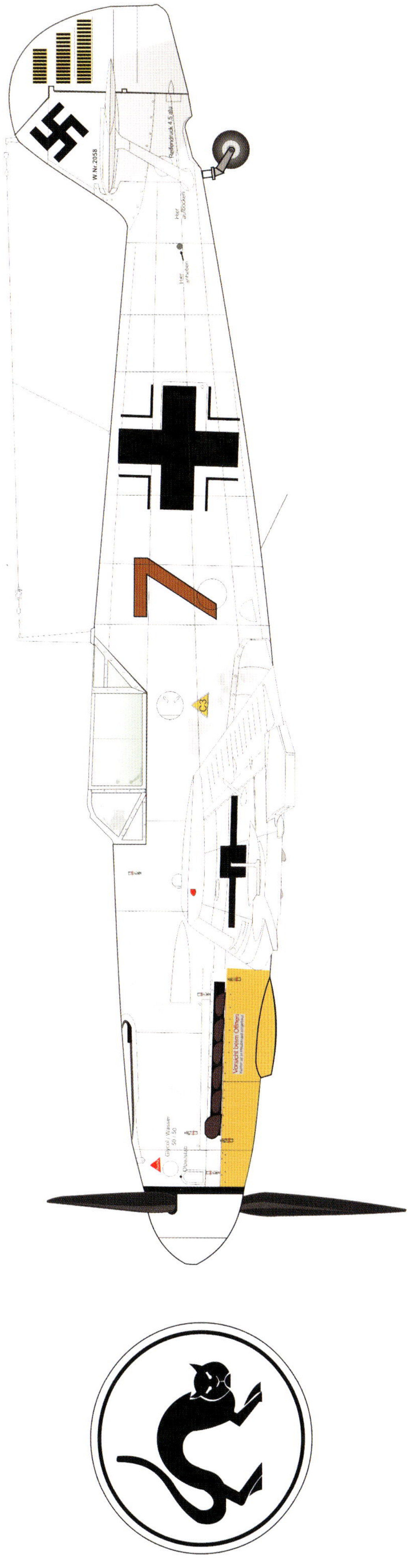

Bf 109F-4 3./JG 51, 'Yellow 7' flown by Oberleutnant Heinrich Kraft in winter camouflage.

Bf 109F-4 in North Africa, 'White Chevron A' of Werner Schroer, JG 27.

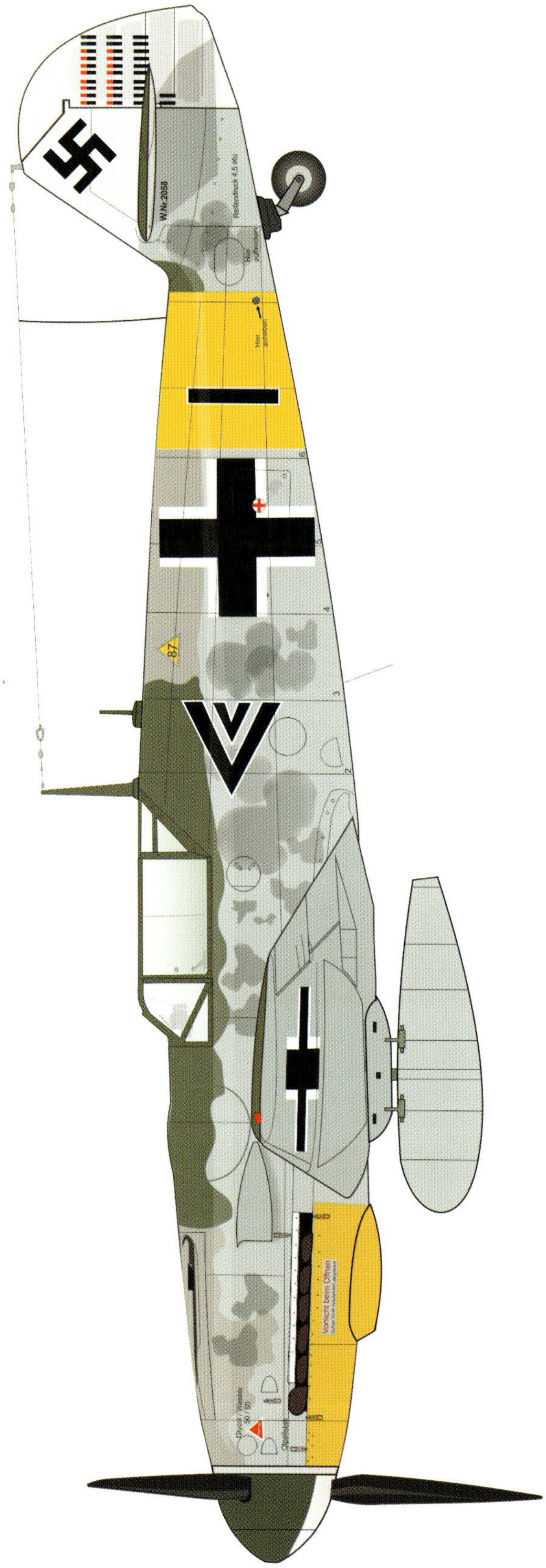

Bf 109G 'Black Chevron' of Anton Hackl, III./JG 11 in mid-war camouflage scheme.

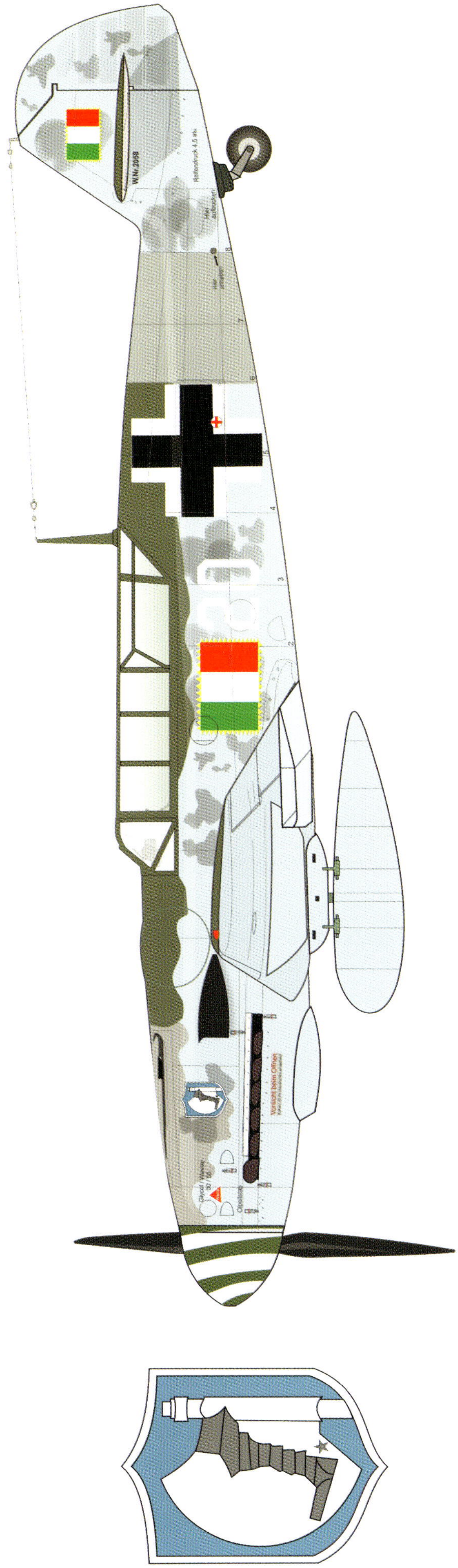

Bf 109G-12/R3 two-seater, Italian ANR, II Gruppo Caccia, 'White 20'.

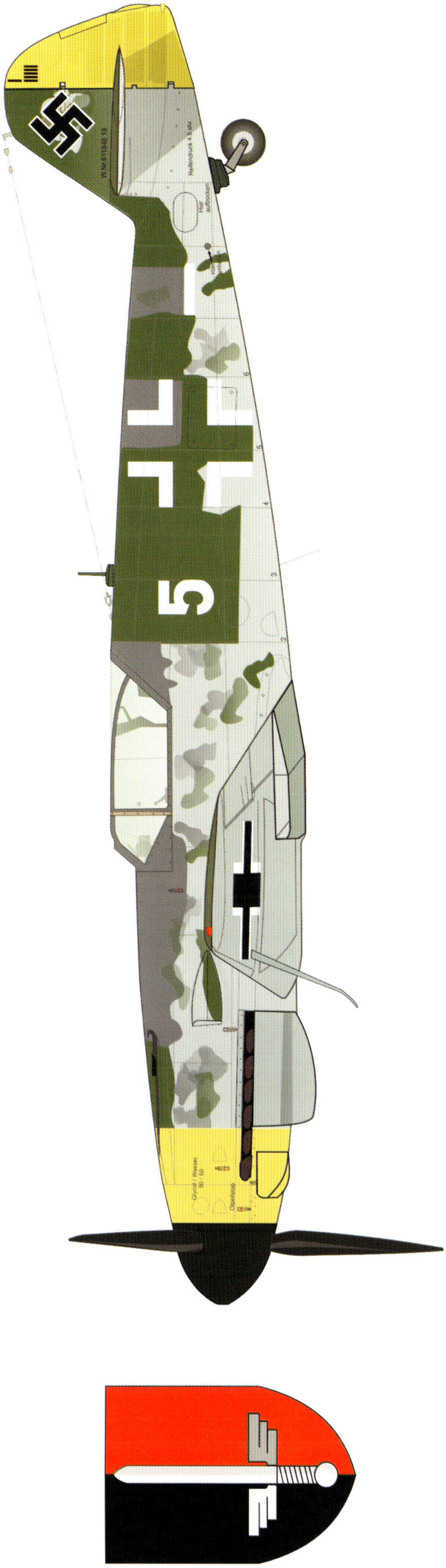

Bf 109G-10/U2 late war, 'White 5' of II./JG 52.

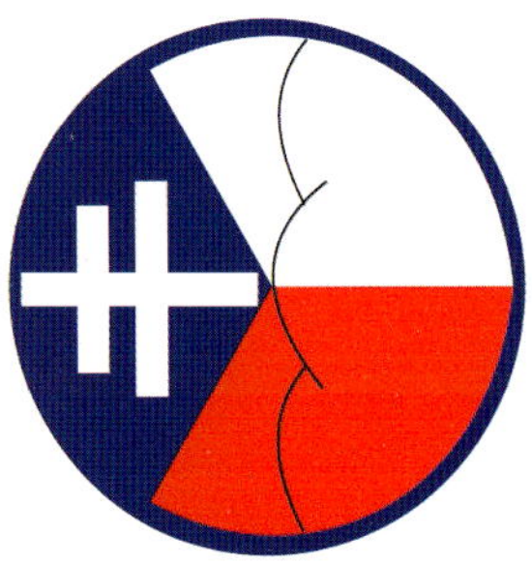

Bf 109D 'White 72' of 5 (Slovak)./Jagdgruppe Drontheim.

Romanian Bf 109G-2/R6, 'White 5', of Grupul 7.

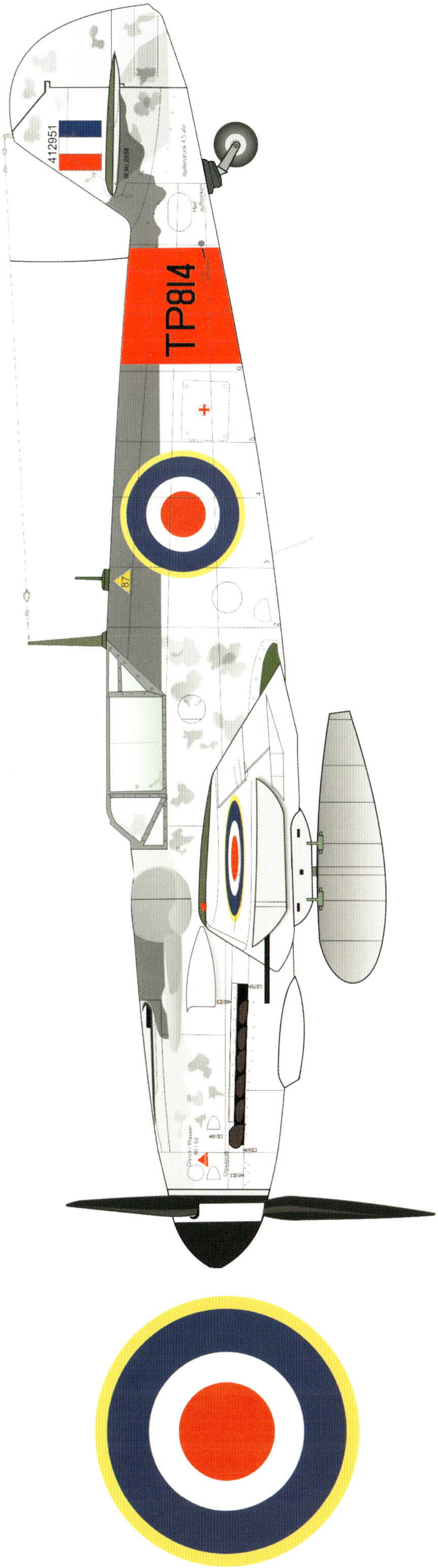

Captured example, Bf 109G-6/U2 in RAF markings, RAE Farnborough.

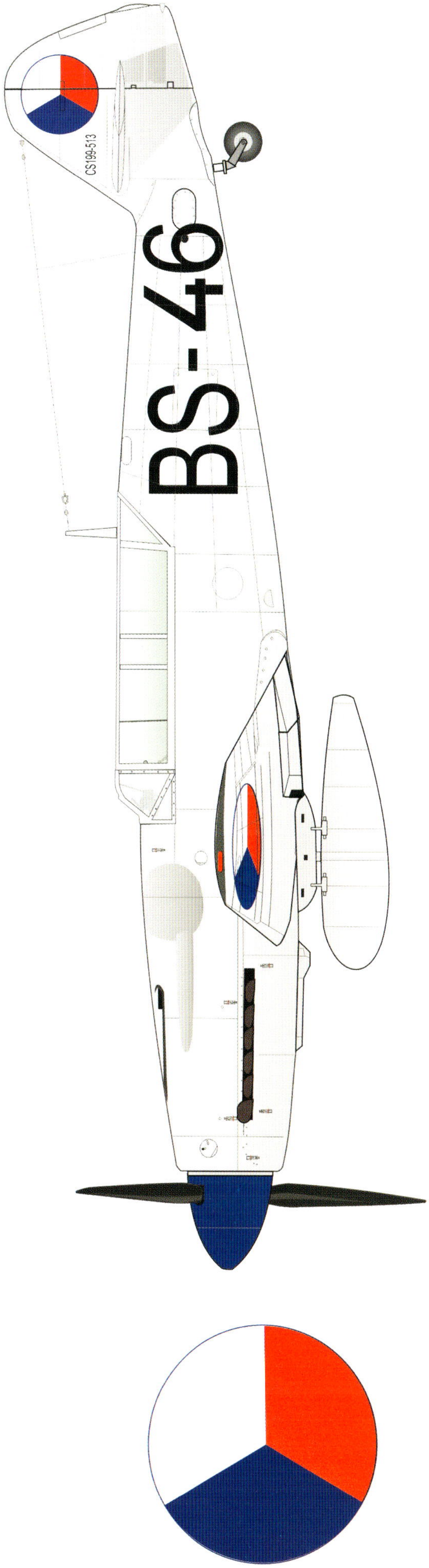

Two-seat Avia CS-199 of the post-war Czech air force, BS-46 of 18th Aviation Regiment.

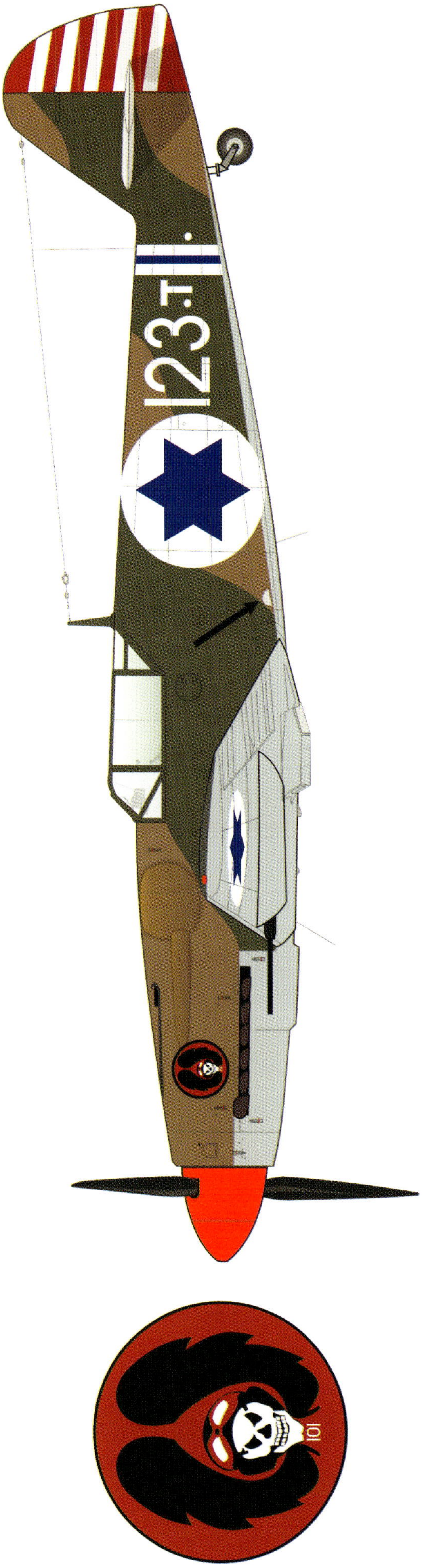

Avia S-199 Mezek (Mule) of 101 Squadron, Israeli Air Force.

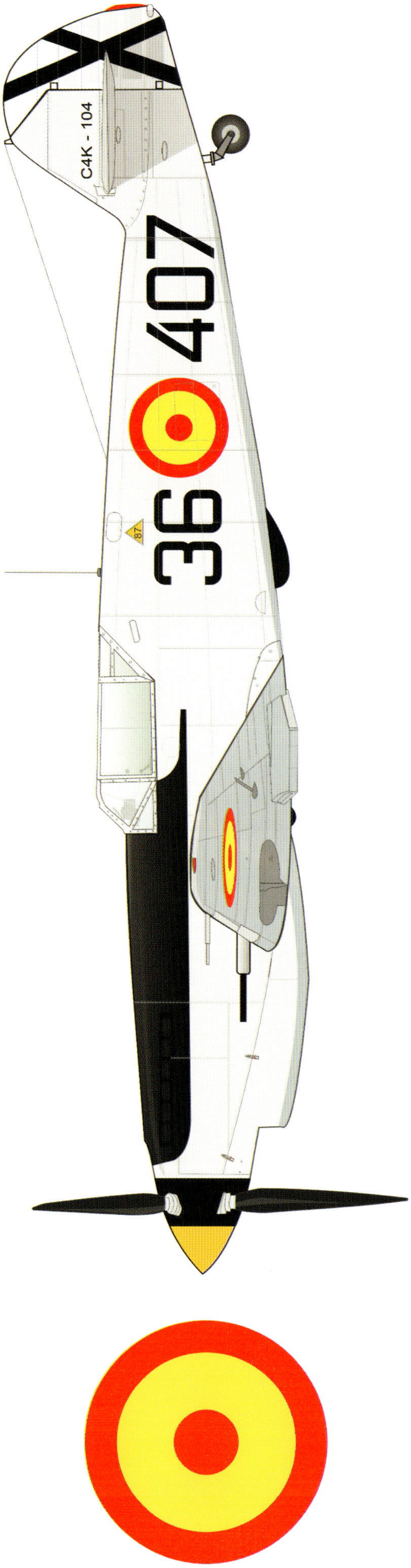

Hispano HA 1112-M1L Buchón, 36-407 of Ala 36, Spanish Air Force.

Modelling the Bf 109

ACADEMY

Academy is a Korean plastic model company that manufactures Messerschmitt kits in 1/48 and 1/72 scale. A variety of variants is offered in both scales.

Modeller **Dan Lee** offers this review of its 1/48 K-4:

This Academy/Hobbycraft edition contains Cartograph decals which replace the terrible Academy ones. It has three metal-detail parts: pitot tube and two gun barrels for the fuselage guns. The markings are for the well-known Red Tulip'ed 'Black 4' of JG52. I used this kit as is except for the cockpit which I replaced with a True details K-4 cockpit. The latter took quite a bit of sanding down but once cleaned up the parts glued together nicely. I added some thin plastic card strips to add some detail that was missing in the wheel wells. Once the glue had cured I spent quite a bit of time filling and sanding to remove all the seams. The plane was primed with Tamiya RLM02 but the rest is painted with Poly Scale: the mottling didn't work out as planned and I believe it is the paint that was the cause of this problem and some touching up was necessary. Based on previous experience with tulip decals and decals on complex shapes in general, I decided to paint the red tulips instead of using the kit decals. I have also found that the colour on the decals tends to be slightly different to the paint I use. It took a lot of careful masking and measuring to get the first masks into position. I did two Tulips at a time and

© Dan Lee

© Dan Lee

started with the white. The Red (RLM 23) was next. I used Tamiya tape because I can see through it and it allowed me to align each piece so that there was a uniform thickness of white. The prop hub parts were sprayed at the same time. Once it was dry, I sprayed on a couple of coats of Tamiya Gloss in preparation for the decals. Apparently 'Black 4' was in relatively good condition when it was captured so I only applied a thin watercolour wash and some exhaust/gunfire stains using the Tamiya Weathering set. This K-4 model is an easy kit to build even with the TD cockpit. It has some accuracy issues and some of the detail is very simplistic, but not enough to detract from building the kit and the metal parts are a nice touch.

The Academy E-3/4 kit represents the Messerschmitt flown by Luftwaffe ace, Heinrich 'Heinz' Bär. Modeller **Francisco Santoro** reviews this 1/48 E-3 kit thus:

Some tips for the modeller to note regarding the construction is the alignment of the control panel can be tricky and the cockpit fit is complicated, so take your time. It is also better to wait for the fuselage to be glued together before you add the radiator, because of the lack of locating tabs for it. With regards to the cowling, don´t glue the machine guns, leave them in their sprue and paint them as a separate item. Something which I also recommend is gluing the propeller shaft to the prop retainer, leaving it to dry, removing it, and then leaving it for a future assembly stage. Thanks to the tight fit of the cowling in its place, there is no need to glue it, you can paint the entire plane, remove it, add the machine guns and then the propeller and leave it like that. Something that distinguished the E-3 from the E-1 is the heavy machine gun bulges on the undersides of the wing. They do not come with alignment pins, you will have to eyeball the proper location for them. The wing machine guns need to have holes opened for their attachment, these are flashed areas on the wings. Before gluing the wings together, paint in RLM 02 the parts of the upper wings that are over the wheel wells, and glue the radiators to the one piece wing (one of them may not fit and will have to be lightly trimmed). With the wings glued and dried, it is time to glue them to the fuselage. This is the tricky fit. I couldn´t manage to get it to be straight and the bulkhead in which the rudder pedals are glued didn't allow me to glue the wings properly, so I sanded the bulkhead until the wings could be fitted. Gluing the flaps in a drop position was difficult as there is no solid surface on which to glue them except for the little contact point between the flaps, the lower wing and the fuselage. There are decals for the camouflage but I chose to paint it. I experienced some problems with the colour RLM 65 (Revell Matt 49) covering the fuselage, perhaps owing to the blue plastic and when I glued on the struts I noticed they were longer than they should have been so I had to cut and trim them. The most tedious part was sanding the paint ridges left by the brush: I used wet sandpaper of 1200 grade. A highlight of this kit is the decals, they are top quality and need no preparation to add. A nice, simple kit that yields a fine replica.

© Francisco Santoro

© Francisco Santoro

The G-6 was the most-produced Bf 109 variant of the war and **Jonathan Prestidge** reviews the 1/48 Academy kit:

This is a re-boxed Hobbycraft kit with easy to follow instructions and much better decals. Academy's Bf 109 series is cleanly moulded with a simple cockpit. The surface detail is engraved but basic and there are no posable control surfaces (slats, flaps, rudder, etc.). The clear parts are a bit of a let down in that they don't fit well – the centre section being too short vertically and too narrow. The shape of the finished kit looks true to the prototype, though I admit to not being a rivet counter. Parts to model a Bf 109G-5 are also included in the kit. The G-5 was essentially a pressurized G-6. Externally, the G-5 had a protrusion from the starboard side "bump" that covered the pressurization compressor. Photos also show dual-pane cockpit glass and a rubber seal around the rear of the engine cowling. The decals in the kit are nicely printed with complete stencils and markings for two aircraft: a G-6 flown by Oberleutnant Erich Hartmann during October 1943 in Russia, and one flown by Oberleutnant Emil Klade during January 1944 in Greece.

Starting with the cockpit, I added an Eduard P.E. seatbelt and an oxygen line made from twist-tie wire. With the cockpit painted and complete, I closed up the fuselage. By gluing the upper wings to the fuselage, I got a great wing-to-fuselage join (no sanding and filing in this often tricky spot). The rest of the airframe was then assembled. The fit was good, needing just a bit of putty in the seams. Next came sanding around the cockpit area to get a better fit for the canopy. I added a thin strip of styrene to the top of the cockpit sills so the canopy fit flush when closed. I also made a few tweaks to the engine cowl in the pursuit of accuracy. The kit parts have the cowl hinge end where the machine guns exit the top decking, which is incorrect. I used a thin trimming of styrene to replicate the rest of the hinge, terminating it between the gun blisters. Once it was attached, I softened it with liquid cement and notched it with the back of an Exacto blade. Using a Hasegawa G-6 as a guide, I filled in and rescribed a

© Jonathan Prestidge

© Jonathan Prestidge

few panel lines on the cowl as well. I added a belly tank pirated from an Eduard 109. It fit with minor tweaking. I then sanded and polished the airframe prior to painting.

Feeling that Hartmann's Bf 109 has been over-modeled, I searched the internet for a photograph of the aircraft I wanted my model to depict. I found several photos of all-blue (RLM 76) G-5s on the Eastern front and decided to model 'White 4'. I had the stencils I needed in the kit decals, so I only had to find a white 4 and the correct upper-wing crosses in the decal dungeon. I added a swastika to the tail of the model that was not shown in the photo (they were commonly edited out of wartime photos). Since the markings of 'White 4' in the photo were otherwise standard, I left it on (builder's prerogative). Also, I placed a white stripe on the spinner that may or may not have been there. It was impossible to see the spinner in the photos I could find. The swirling stripe was very common on German aircraft and I liked it (again builder's prerogative). Weathering was done with pastels applied with a closely cropped paintbrush.

To me there is something enjoyable about trying to build an older kit well – I like the challenge. The finished kit looks good on the shelf. The simple colour scheme really shows off the sinister lines of the Bf 109. Real 109s have slats and flaps opened up when on the ground and the lack of these features is the main failing of this kit. Currently there are better kits of the Bf 109G. The Hasegawa and Eduard offerings are much nicer and more accurate. They are also more complex and can be much more expensive. If you can find the Academy kit cheap or have one already then it is a viable option. It is well suited to newer modelers due to its simplicity.

© Jonathan Prestidge

© Jonathan Prestidge

© Jonathan Prestidge

AIRFIX

Airfix offers a variety of Messerschmitt Bf 109 kits and aftermarket products. There is a strong focus on the Bf 109E in terms of variants, colour schemes and scales including 1/72, 1/48 and 1/24. The Bf109E-4 1/72 is a 64-piece, model that is suitable for all ages. It fits together snuggly so no filler is needed and has surprising detail in the engine and cockpit for such a small model. Lovely model with great decals. The Messerschmitt Bf109E-4/N Trop 1/48 and Messerschmitt Bf109E-4/E-1 are pegged as a level 2 build and has 107 parts. It adds to what has gone before in terms of the E-1, E-3 and E-7 (a 60-piece model for beginners or the advanced modeller looking for a quicker, simpler build) and features two colour schemes: the aircraft flown by Major Eduard Neumann, 1./JG27, North Africa, 1941-42 and the aircraft (allegedly) flown by Lieutenant Peter-Paul Steindl, Stab II./JG54, Arad, Romania, March 1941. The Messerschmitt Bf109E-4/E-3 1/24 features 146 parts but is now more difficult to purchase. Over the years Airfix has released combinations of most variants in most scales and for most abilities, this includes the Messerschmitt Bf 109G-6 1/72 which is a quick, simple build that is perfect for beginners – skill level 1 – due to straight forward instructions and a low parts count, 41 in total. A good fit with two good decal schemes. The cockpit complexity is disappointing for the more advanced modeller as it is very basic, but an aftermarket cockpit kit is available.

© Scott van Aken

© Scott van Aken

Airfix Bf 109E-4 1/72 modelled and reviewed by **Scott van Aken**:
This is an all new tool 1/72 kit designed to replace the older moulding and looking very much like their 1/48 release; the engraved panel lines seem to be more subdued. The kit has an engine block of sorts moulded in with the fuselage halves, like you will find with the Tamiya kit. (I added some photo etch seat belts from Eduard over the ones molded into the seat.) There is also a pilot if you wish one. There are separate flaps that can be modelled in the down position and Airfix has included the aileron mass balances. Also separate is the rudder, which you could place at an angle as the leading edge of the rudder is rounded. The canopy can be built in the open position and the three-piece construct is quite clear with well defined frames. Typical of Airfix kits, the gear can be built up, though no stand is included. Both the main wheels and tail wheel have a flat spot on them. This kit only models a Battle of Britain 109E-4. Markings are for a single aircraft as flown by Franz von Werra during August 1940 with II./JG 3. There is no mottling on this so brush painters will like it. There is no swastika either so you will need to rob your spares bin for a historically accurate finish. I should mention that the instrument panel is a decal, which is pretty much the norm for this scale. They are oversize by about 20 percent. It is a very satisfying kit and especially at the most reasonable price that Airfix asks for this. I can see a lot of these being built by 109 fans and I would very much like to see an E-3 and E-7 included in their catalogue. I found that some of the parts were quite fragile while others were a very tight fit. It makes me think that these kits would not be all that suitable for children who have little experience with kits as they will break a lot of parts during assembly. I am sure the aftermarket folk will be doing a cockpit for this one in the near future and I have to say that while not quite as nice as the Tamiya and other early 109 kits, it is still one that makes into a most acceptable kit and does so for well under half the price of the Japanese version.

© Scott van Aken

© Scott van Aken

© Mark Mallinson

© Mark Mallinson

Mark Mallinson comments on the Airfix Bf 109E-3 1/24, JG26, flown by Adolf Galland in autumn 1940. With many good references on the Emil at my disposal, I decided to make whatever adjustments the kit required to accurately represent this mainstay of the Luftwaffe. Some of the modifications include the adjustment of the flaps, I wanted them down, while the Airfix model is moulded up; the wheel wells and oleo tunnels were nothing more than open holes in the bottoms of the wings; I hollowed-out gun barrels, opened engine exhausts and air intakes; I rescribed the panel lines missing from the lower fuselage center section; added to the landing gear; simulated hydraulic lines and straps; Waldron seat belts, dial gages and an oxygen hose were added to the cockpit interior along with some Model Master chrome dry brushing in high wear areas. The end result is a BIG hunk of plastic, which will grab the attention of anyone familiar with the Battle of Britain.

© Mark Mallinson

ALLEY CAT

Frank Reynolds shares his views on a Bf 109D conversion kit in 1/32 scale:

Alley Cat do around ten major 109 conversion sets in 1/32 scale and about as many minor ones. This one is specifically marketed as a Swiss version. Eduard's Bf109E-1 is the recommended donor kit but an E-3 will do with minor adjustments to the wings, by deleting the small under wing gun blisters. The intention of this build was to simply go for an example demonstrating the maximum amount of bright colouring displayed on a Swiss 109. Alley cat's pale grey resin parts with their subtly engraved surfaces are a good match for Eduard's plastic. The instructions provide a critical and excellent explanation of how to modify the Eduard parts. This is an exercise in backdating a BF109E by deleting the underwing radiators, providing a two-bladed propeller and replacing the DB601 engine with a Junkers Jumo 210. A note regarding the construction: when cutting away the parts of Eduard plastic that are not required, the one-piece lower wing panels require the removal of the prominent radiator assemblies and a large section at the leading edge of the centre section to accommodate the new chin radiator housing. This last cut is perilously close to the landing gear bays but with care it can be done. Also, the modified wing section flops around noticeably and this is a good time to glue in the resin lower wing inserts. Unsure as to how well white decal crosses would show up on red paintwork I used Montex Super Masks for a Swiss BF 109E, which have the required proportions and sprayed the national insignia. Alley Cat provides a well-designed product that is relatively easy to use and this could serve as a first attempt at a resin conversion. Eduard's Bf109s are of consistently good quality and provide a fuss-free build and their instructions helpfully include detailed notes on the colours of individual cockpit parts. I was happy with the performance of the Montex masks and this might encourage me to try a more ambitious project with them.

© Frank Reynolds

© Frank Reynolds

© Frank Reynolds

© Frank Reynolds

© Frank Reynolds

EDUARD

This Czechoslovakian scale model company offered two kits in 1/144 scale, a Bf 109F and a 109G however both have been discontinued by the manufacturer but are occasionally available via other sources. In 1/32 scale Eduard has a full range of the E variant in various colour schemes with a variety of markings. Their 'over the Balkan Peninsular', E-7 trop and Profipack E-1 have been discontinued but again may be found floating around other sources. Their 1/48 scale products cover a range of E, F and G kits. Eduard does not offer 1/72 scale models.

Scott Lyle offers this review to modellers of the 1/48 scale E-4:
Some years ago Eduard launched an all new line of 1/32 Emils that have been generally well received, albeit not without some gnashing of teeth. Recently it started a new line of 1/48 Emils, the first offering being an E-1 followed by a Royal Class release that provided all of the parts needed to build two Emils in either E-1, E-3, E-4, or E-7 guises. This kit is thus their third 1/48 Emil release, and upon opening the box, there is a lot to like. This kit includes two frets of photo etch (including one colour set which includes precisely printed instrument panels, seat belts, and cockpit sidewall details), yellow kabuki tape, cockpit masks and two sheets of decals: one for stencils and one for the markings for five different Bf 109E-4s. Amongst those plastic sprues are the parts to build a nicely detailed DB601a engine and the machine gun bay above it, as well as the separate cowling panels needed to display them open if desired. Other options include separate

© Scott Lyle

© Scott Lyle

leading edge extensions, flaps, ailerons, and the rudder. Two different windscreens are included, as well as two different prop spinners. The fuselage and wing surfaces are sublimely moulded, with row after row of tiny, recessed rivet heads that should look great under a coat of paint and some weathering. I decided to build my Emil as a replica of Adolf Galland's famous Werknummer #5819. When constructing the engine you need to decide if yours is going to be buttoned up or open, I went for the former but must caution you to follow the instructions carefully as the engine serves primarily to hold the exhaust stubs in place (which have noticeable ribs moulded onto them – do not file those off)! Closing up the fuselage halves required some attention as you have to make sure all of those items line up nicely as well as trap the engine in such a way that the exhaust stubs snake through their respective slots in the fuselage halves. Ultimately the fit is very good, but make sure you do some test-fitting beforehand. The only real seam work I did on the fuselage was on the underside of the nose. Attaching the cowling panels around the engine is fiddly, but look realistic. Eduard provides hollow gun barrel stubs for the nose and wings so there's no need to drill them out. Galland's 5819 had a good amount of RLM 02/71 mottling all over the RLM 65 Light Blue, so to I replicated that using the kit's instructions as a guide. I also had to mask off a portion of the rudder and spray that with my RLM 65 mix to display Galland's kill markings. The kit's decals behaved beautifully. Regarding the final weathering I diluted the Flat Finish with just a few drops of Lacquer Thinner and then used the Turquoise Aztec tip instead of the Beige tip that I usually use. I found the results excellent with this technique – the Flat Finish sprayed more finely and smoothly than before. I'll be using the Turquoise tip for this task from now on. This kit is an absolute gem. With all that Eduard provides in the box, you won't need to buy a single aftermarket item, save for maybe decals. The level of detail is very high and the quality of the moulded surfaces is superb.

© Scott Lyle

© Scott Lyle

© Scott Lyle

© Scott Lyle

© Scott Lyle

HASEGAWA

Hasegawa offers huge variety of 109s: as a Combo kit the E-3 Condor Legion with a HE 51B-1. In offers 1/48, 1/32 and two 1/72 Limited Editions. The 1/48s are the E-4 JG77 Blitz, F-2 Barbarossa, F-4/B JG53 and F-4 TROP/R1, the G-6 and G-15 are both offered as the Hartmann as well as three other Limited G-6s: the Graf, Arcadia and 'Shidenkai no Maki'. In 1/32 scale Limited Editions modellers have a choice of numerous F-4s: F-4B 'Jabo' or 'Priller', F-6U or 'Juutilainen' (with figure) and finally in the K-4. Two Limited Edition 1/72 kits are available: the E-7 as a Combo with a FW 190A-5 Japanese Army and the G-6 in Finnish Air Force colours. Standard kits are limited to 1/32 scale and include an E, F-4TROP, G-6 and G-10. Hasegawa produce plastic models and are based in japan, making Tamiya their main competitor, although they do not offer as large a range as Tamiya does.

© Denis Jankowski

© Denis Jankowski

Denis Jankowski's Messerschmitt Bf 109 E-4 'Helmut Wick' is based on a Hasegawa 1/32. Helmut Paul Emil Wick (5 August 1915) was a fighter ace and the fourth recipient of the Knight's Cross of the Iron Cross with Oak Leaves of Nazi Germany, the nation's highest military decoration at the time. He was shot down claiming his 55th aerial victory by a Spitfire on 28 November 1940.

A tremendous challenge, despite 20-plus years of model making as I found this kit very inaccurate. One of the biggest problems was the engine, DB 601, of which very few original parts were eventually used. The cockpit, landing gear, engine covers, air intakes, were all highly improved upon. This built took 18 months and it was very hard to find good aftermarkets for this kit. This problem compelled me to turn this kit into a one of kind model. I've created approximately 1,200 parts from scratch, paying attention even to the letter 'N' on the engine block – related to the compression rate (the fuel had its octane raised from 6.9 to 8.2 on this model) – to cockpit details such as the rear of the panel. Despite the tremendous amount of work it took, it also gave me confidence and skills to attempt more challenging works in the future.

© Denis Jankowski

Modeller **Scott Lyle** makes these observations about the 1/48 G-6 Erich Hartmann kit:

This is a well-chronicl ed model. It is moulded in light grey plastic and is of a very high quality with finely recessed panel lines and a nicely detailed cockpit. Construction of this kit was quick and smooth. I added a few parts to the model to increase the level of detail. I used an Eduard Zoom Color Photo Etch set to enhance the instrument panel and cockpit area. An 'Erla Haube' canopy was sourced from Squadron, and an Eagle Parts resin spinner was added. I also used a set of resin exhausts from Ultracast. It is a rapid, pleasant build that presents no problems. I can see why it such a popular kit, and also why many modellers enjoy building their own *Gruppe* of Bf 109s.

© Scott Lyle

© Scott Lyle

© Scott Lyle

© Scott Lyle

© Scott Lyle

Frank Reynolds offers his 1/32 G-14 Hartmann, prefacing the kit detail with this history: One pilot forever associated with later model Bf109s is Erich 'Bubi' Hartman. His aircraft are much beloved of kit and decal manufacturers due to the distinctive 'Black Tulip' nose markings that he adopted when a senior officer in the Luftwaffe. He had a remarkable career as a combat pilot between 1942 and 1945, being credited with 352 kills, all but seven being Soviet aircraft. At the end of the Second World War he was imprisoned in the USSR for ten years and upon his release joined the newly formed West German Luftwaffe, where his distinctive Black Tulip insignia was worn of the F-86s of JG 71 – the Richtofen Squadron.

I chose to trust Hasegawa entirely with this one by relying on what was in the box and using minimal aftermarket. The extra interest would come in trying to create the winter colour scheme. During construction I came upon an anomaly in that the flaps to the rear edge of the wings are moulded with inset hinges so that they can be displayed open. However, this is at odds with the fixed ailerons, elevators and rudder which are moulded integrally with the adjacent flying surfaces, so the hinges were trimmed away and the flap assemblies cemented closed up. Similarly the leading edge slats were trimmed and cemented closed. I had a decals disaster. Perhaps distracted by how straightforward the build had been thus far I was happily floating the decals into place, each with the help of some Micro Set when I decided that the larger crosses could be hurried along with a liberal dose of Micro Sol. I watched in horror as the large crosses to the upper wings shrivelled, cracked and crazed. The rest of the decals had gone on without fuss so the Micro Sol wasn't needed. The black petals for the nose are supplied as a linked trio for the cowl sides and I found it easier to cut them apart and apply each one separately, especially around the engine exhausts, even these settled into place without the use of Micro. I completed the installation of all the available decals and contemplated how to put things right. It was fortunate that the second option on Hasegawa's decal sheet features outline white crosses of the correct size so they were used as a pattern to build up a Tamiya tape mask on each upper wing which permitted a solid cross to be sprayed in grey – I used Tamiya XF-77 IJN Grey. The white outline

© Frank Reynolds

© Frank Reynolds

crosses were cut into quarters and each chevron-shaped section juggled onto the new grey painted cross, the outline crosses having been split up to allow for any imperfections in the geometry of my masking. This kit is expensive but pricing aside, if you want a relaxed and worry-free build of a 109, grab this one. This G-14 has an option that is free from the challenges of mottling the camouflage and the white upper surfaces can be finished pristine or worn to suit individual tastes. Unless you suffer from Advanced Modeller Syndrome you surely cannot go wrong. With virtually no need for filler and no gimmicks, it is an ideal way to practice the pure pleasure of modelling.

© Frank Reynolds

© Frank Reynolds

© Frank Reynolds

HELLER

Modeller **Brian R. Baker**:

Heller is a French company that began production of an excellent series of plastic aircraft models in 1957. Although they have built some kits in other scales, the majority of their offerings are in 1/72 scale. They have produced kits of all of the major Bf-109 variants, including the Bf-109B/C, Bf-109E, Bf-109F, Bf-109G and Bf-109K. All kits appear to have been produced from the middle sixties, and all have the same level of moulding and detail. Heller is one of the few producers to offer the earliest version of the Bf-109, the Jumo-powered Bf-109B and Bf-109C variants. These could also be converted to the Bf-109D with little effort, as the airframes of all of these are almost identical.

The Bf-109B/C kit is well moulded, and accurate in outline. The kit has fine raised panel lines, and moderate cockpit detail. The canopy is moulded in three pieces, so you can leave it open to show the cockpit detail. Two props are provided, the wooden prop used on early models, and the metal prop installed on later C and D models. The instructions are printed on a single sheet of typing paper, and include a parts' list (but no sprue diagram), an exploded assembly drawing, and colour and marking details for two versions. The decal sheet has markings for a Condor Legion Bf-109B-1 and a Luftwaffe Bf-109C-1 of 9/ZG26. Aftermarket decals are available for other aircraft. Construction is easy, and any modeller of moderate skill levels should have no trouble with it. The cockpit interior should be assembled and detailed first, followed by the fuselage and wing assembly. Very little filler is needed, and once basic assembly is completed, major painting can be done. Following this, detail parts, such as the landing gear, tail bracing struts and propeller, can be installed. After a coat

Bf-109B-1 Condor Legion.

Bf-109D-1 1/JG127.

Bf-109E-1 7/JG51

of gloss lacquer to ensure decal adhesion, decals can be applied. This kit is inexpensive and easy to construct. They are often available at low prices at kit swapping sessions held by various modelling clubs, as well as at the better hobby shops.

Bf-109G-14 7/JG52.

© Brian R. Baker

Bf-109G-14AS 4/JG5.

© Brian R. Baker

Bf-109K-4 1/JG77.

© Brian R. Baker

REVELL

Revell offers the full range of Bf 109 variants in 1/32, 1/48 and 1/72 scale. It even offers two kits in 1/144 for the Bf 109E. The popular range of markings and colour schemes that most scale model kit manufacturers offer is available through Revell as well.

Frank Reynolds reviews the G-10 Erla variant:
The Erla provides an excellent canvas for a rich variety of colour schemes, and aftermarket decal producers have given the modelling community a good choice – with the exception of one. I have a photo of the intriguing Me109G-10 of 15/JG.52 which was surrendered to US forces by its Croatian pilot at Falconara, Italy, in April 1945. The 15th Staffel of JG52 was composed of Croatian Air Force personnel, their aircraft carried the distinctive Cross of King Svonomir as a national insignia and the tail carries a red and white chequered shield that in the 21st century is more recognisable as the national colours of Croatia. This colour scheme has been on my modelling bucket list for 40 years while I waited for the resources to produce this model, looking for an appropriate airframe and the right national insignia. Even so I had to stray into the relatively unknown World of Montex's vinyl masks, since I could not find this

© Frank Reynolds

© Frank Reynolds

© Frank Reynolds

© Frank Reynolds

scheme on a currently available decal sheet. Since the colour and markings were the crux of this project I made a radical change from my normal style of build: the national insignia would be painted first. Although Montex provides a single example of a fuselage cross in decal form printed to resemble damaged paintwork, I rejected that option since I did not want the problem of trying to match the density of painted colour on the other crosses to the ink of the decal and in any event Montex provides masks for all six crosses. Next I turned to the installation of the masks and I found on-line tutorials to be really useful. I had long wondered how to lift multi-part insignia from the backing sheet without distorting them or leaving some parts behind and Montex have some good advice. The decals mainly consisted of Luftwaffe stencilling from the kit's decal sheet, Montex's contribution being confined to the red and white shield on the tail, the Ram's head insignia under the cockpit and a small serial number. This particular aircraft required a small teardrop-shaped bulge in the lower front corners of the engine cowl. For a 1/32 fighter project, the price was remarkably low, including the masks. This is my second attempt at Montex masks with a satisfactory result. Revell's 109G-10 offers has much scope for those who like to go to town with aftermarket and super detailing, yet it is a satisfying build with minimal alteration for those who are looking for something simpler.

TRUMPETER

As with the other big names Trumpeter has it all when it comes to the Bf 109, the Es, the Fs, the Gs and the late K variants, in all their colour schemes and even in service with other air forces. Trumpeter is a Chinese company that manufactures plastic-injection moulding model kits. It produces kits of airplanes in 1/144, 1/72, 1/48, 1/32 and 1/24 scale. The kits in the larger scales are generally highly detailed and include metal parts, while the smaller scale kits usually are rather simple.

Richard Reynolds reviews its 1/32 G-2 with Finish Air Force colour and markings: The kit is beautifully detailed and the surface detail is crisp displaying fine panel lines and rivet detail. The fuselage detail includes all of the internal ribbing which enhances the detail even when an after-market cockpit is used. The instrument panel was supplied with an acetate instrument film; I found the instrument dials to be too dark and elected to replace them with Airscales 1/32 WWII Generic Luftwaffe instrument dial decals. . The only addition that I made were a pair of MG 131's over the engine in resin by Quickboost as the kit supplied MGs were very basic. Unfortunately the effect of the detailed engine would be lost as I had elected to model the aircraft with the engine covers closed. Nevertheless, should you wish to display the Bf 109G-2 with the engine covers open the kit supplied DB 605 is excellent. Two colour

options are available in the kit, however I decided to finish it as a Finnish Air Force example. I chose Techmod's 1/32 Messerschmitt Bf 109G-2 in Finnish service decals. This makes a well detailed example of the Messerschmitt Bf 109G. The comprehensive engine, cockpit and the inclusion of the slats, flaps and radiators coupled with the ease of construction builds a fine example of this iconic aircraft.

ZVEZDA

Darren Wilks comments on a Zvezda F-2 build:

This is Zvezda's Bf 109F-2 Kit in 1/48 scale built entirely out of the box apart from Eduard steel seatbelts. Until the advent of the Eduard range of BF109 Fs this kit and the F -really were the benchmark of 1/48 109 Fs on the market. The kit features a full engine if you choose to show it off as well as finely engraved panel lines and a pilot figure. Also in the box are rustaz packs for underwing cannon gondolas as well as various bomb racks. The kit builds well but does need some time taken due to the full engine that can be on display as well as the multiple piece radiators and flaps. That said I encountered no problems with the build of the kit. The aircraft modelled is that of Johannes Trautloft, the commanding officer of JG 54 on the eastern front these aircraft differed from a lot of Luftwaffe aircraft at the time by having non-standard camouflage schemes. In this case it is believed that the lower surfaces were RLM 76 with RLM 04 yellow and the upper surfaces were captured Russian stocks of brown and dark green.

© Darren Wilks

© Darren Wilks

© Darren Wilks

A selection of 1/32 scale Bf 109 models featuring a variety of colour schemes and markings by **Frank Reynolds**.

Messerschmitt Bf109B-1, 1/J88 Condor Legion, Spain 1937. Eduard Bf 109E kit with Alley Cat resin conversion.

Messerschmitt Bf109E-7 Trop, Luftwaffe 1/JG27 Libya 1941. Eduard kit.

Messerschmitt Bf109E-1, Luftwaffe, 9/JG26, France 1940. Eduard kit.

Messerschmitt Bf109F-4 Trop, Luftwaffe 3/JG27 North Africa 1942. Hasegawa kit.

Messerschmitt Me109G-2/R6, Romanian Air Force 7th Fighter Group, Taganrog 1943. Trumpeter kit.

Messerschmitt Me 109G-6, Royal Hungarian Air Force 101/3 Puma Squadron, 1944. Trumpeter kit.

Messerschmitt Me109G-6/R6 Trop. 150 Grupo Autonomo 1943. Revell kit modified.

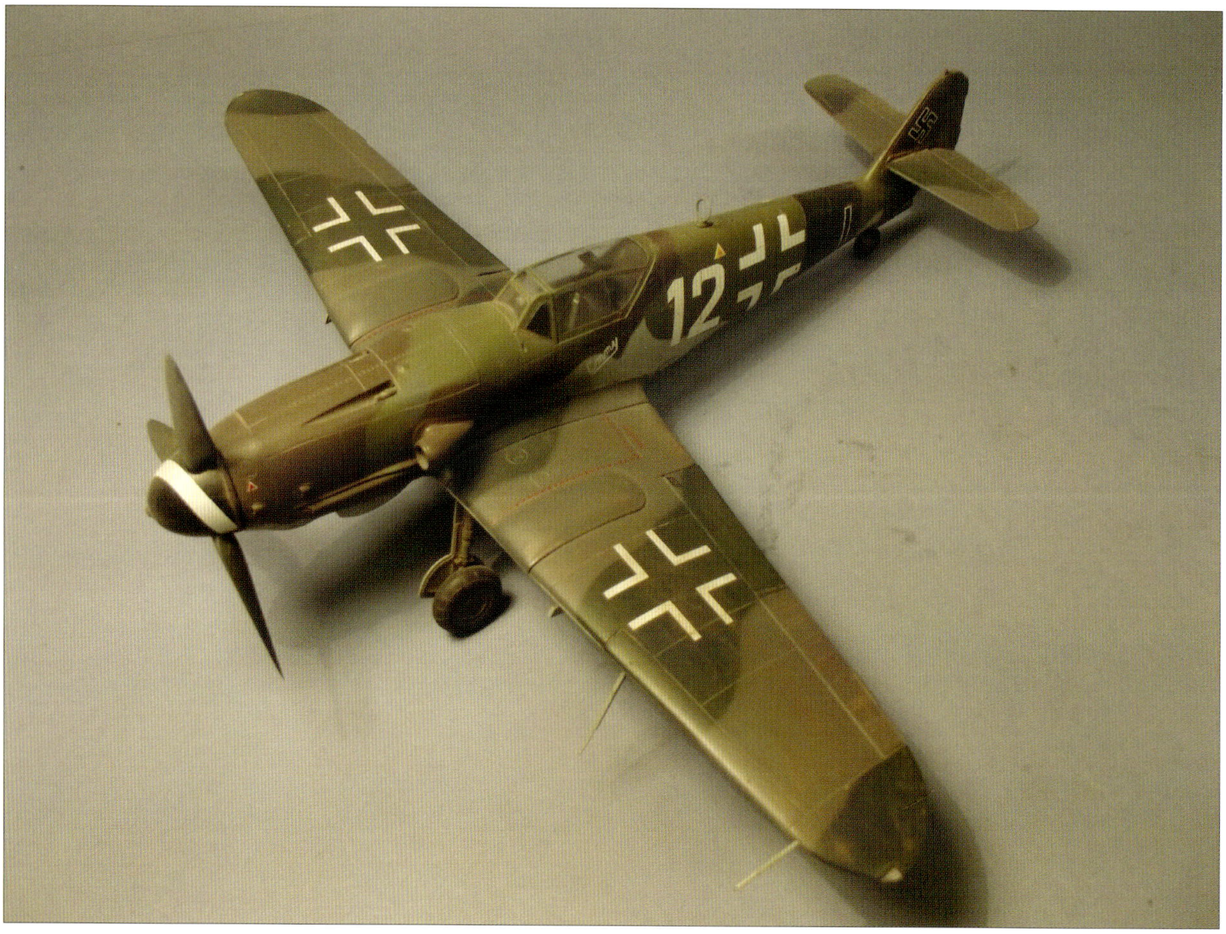

Messerschmitt Me 109K-4 9/JG3 Luftwaffe Germany 1945. Hasegawa kit.

Hispano HA-1112-M1L Spanish Air Force 71e Escuadron, Tenerife 1958. Hasegawa 109G modified with Grey Matter resin conversion.

MODEL SHOWCASE

Trumpeter Bf 109K-4 1/32

Jay Howard

Overall I liked the kit, although I wish Trumpeter had made a few more of the changes that differentiate the K-4 from the G-10. The main item for me would be the starboard side of the cockpit, which is very different on a K-4. I ended up using a spare panel from a Hasegawa K-4. Trumpeter did change the location of the radio access panel on the port side, but it is oddly shaped and needs to be rescribed. I did like their treatment of the tailwheel doors, which are molded separately rather than molded as part of the fuselage, in the open position, on the Hasegawa version. They were typically closed permanently in the field. Ease of assembly and fit are very good on all the Trumpeter 109s that I have built. I did use some aftermarket parts such as BarracudaCast prop blades, spinner, and wheels, G-Factor gear legs, RB Production seatbelts, and Eagle Cal decals. E-Z Line was used for the antenna wire. Some scratch built items were also added including the pitot tube, DF loop, IFF antenna, landing gear indicators, canopy tether, shell ejection chutes, etc. Mr. Color paint overall with a mix of black and brown gouache paint for the exhaust stains.

Messerschmitt Bf 109K-4
1/32
SCALE

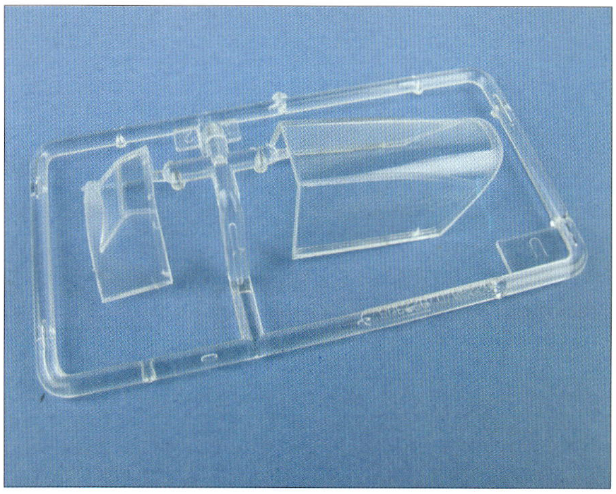

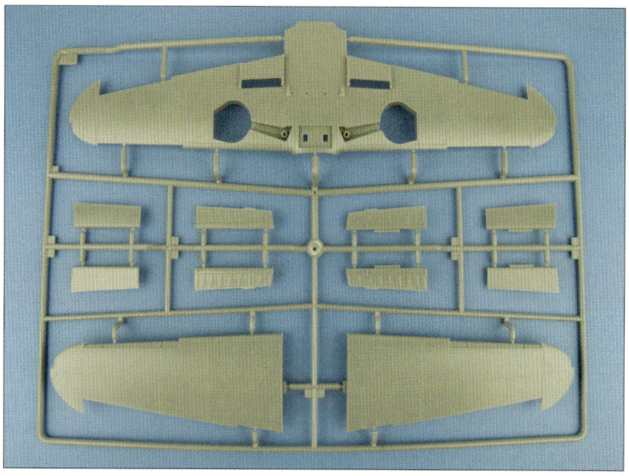

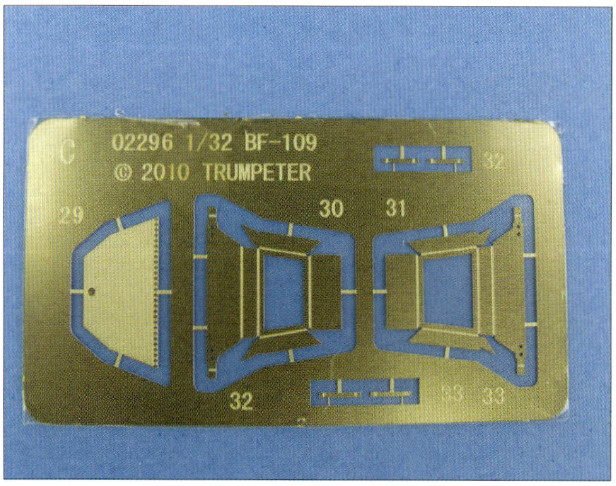

Acknowledgements

Grateful thanks for their time, enthusiasm and generosity go the the talented community of modellers who made those sections of this book the showcase they are. To George Morrison for casting his sharp eye over the profile illustrations and assisting with their corrections so that what is in the book is now a collection of drawings that technically correct. Thank you also too, and this is in alphabetical order as all have been enthusiastic and generous and patient: Brian Baker, Kevin Futter, Jay Howard, Denis Jankowski, Dan Lee, Scott Lyle, Mark Mallinson, Jonathan Prestidge, Frank Reynolds, Richard Reynolds, Francisco Santoro, Scott van Aken and Darren Wilks. Invaluable websites have been modelingmadness.com and largescaleplanes.com.